P9-BYW-282

Color Echoes

In an abandoned cottage garden a dark
pink weigela is echoed by the paler
pink of the rose and this in turn by the
pastel pink of the foxglove. The
foxglove contrasts in form with the
other flowers and, by coincidence,
echoes the shape of a gateway pillar
behind. (England; June)

Color Echoes

Harmonizing Color in the Garden

Written and Photographed by
Pamela J. Harper

Macmillan Publishing Company
New York

Maxwell Macmillan Canada
Toronto

Maxwell Macmillan International
New York   Oxford   Singapore   Sydney

Macmillan Publishing Company   Maxwell Macmillan Canada, Inc.
866 Third Avenue   1200 Eglinton Avenue East
New York, NY 10022   Suite 200
                                      Don Mills, Ontario M3C 3N1

Macmillan Publishing Company is part of the Maxwell Communication Group of Companies.

Library of Congress Cataloging-in-Publication Data
Harper, Pamela.
    Color echoes : harmonizing color in the garden / written and photographed by
  Pamela J. Harper.
        p.   cm.
    Includes index.
    ISBN 0-02-548185-1
    1. Color in gardening.   2. Gardens—Design.   I. Title.
  SB454.3.C64H37   1994
  712'.2—dc20   93-41490
                                                                              CIP

Macmillan books are available at special discounts for bulk purchases for sales promotions, premiums, fund-raising, or educational use. For details, contact:

                    Special Sales Director
                    Macmillan Publishing Company
                    866 Third Avenue
                    New York, NY 10022

10 9 8 7 6 5 4 3 2 1

Printed in the United States of America

DESIGN BY LAURA HOUGH

To my husband, Patrick, who has run the errands, answered the phone, fixed the computer, assessed the relative merits of pictures, and kept his patience while this book was being written.

And to two of the garden owners who have died between writing and publication of this book—John Treasure and Jerry Sedenko. Both will be remembered, with affection and gratitude, by all those with whom they shared their gardens and their plants.

Contents

Introduction   1

Chapter 1: THE LANGUAGE OF COLOR   15

Chapter 2: EXPLORING ECHOES   35

Chapter 3: THE COLORS   97

Chapter 4: THE UNFOLDING OF TWO ECHOES
             BORDERS   191

Index   221

Acknowledgments

Gardening books usually give credit to the photographers who took the pictures. In this case, I took all but one—the beautiful picture of wild lupines taken by my talented nature photographer friend Susan Glascock. Thank you, Sue.

Being a gardener as well as a photographer, I know that taking pictures is the easy part. Most of the credit should go to those whose artistry, hard work, and horticultural skill have set the scene. The names of those who made possible the pictures in this book are shown in the captions. I thank you all.

There are always more pictures than available space. As some get eliminated, I comfort myself with the thought—perhaps next time. Being in a beautiful garden with my camera is my idea of bliss. Whether or not a picture of their garden appears in this book, I extend my deepest gratitude to all who have made me welcome.

Color Echoes

Introduction

Once in a while a catchy phrase or evocative combination of words brings into focus a concept by no means new. "Color Echoes" was the title of a short article I wrote for *Pacific Horticulture* in 1987. The response to it, and to subsequent talks on this topic, has been surprising and gratifying. Becoming aware of echoes clarified for me just what it was I found especially appealing in gardens, groupings, and color combinations, and led me to give more thought to the broad subject of color. It seems to have done the same for others.

Space permitted only cursory discussion of color echoes in my book *Designing with Perennials,* but many have told me it is their favorite part of the book. So now, with the encouragement of friends and of my editor, Pam Hoenig, I am expanding (or expounding!) on this topic, along with the associated topics of coordinated color, contrast, and harmonious combinations.

Thinking about color echoes has added a new dimension to my gardening. I have long been a plant collector, wanting to grow one of everything. If I cannot truthfully claim to be less acquisitive about plants nowadays, at least I now consider not only the plant itself and where it will best grow, but where, and with what companions, it might be placed in order to look its best. I am even, on occasion, able to resist a tempting catalogue description, or to say "No, thank you" to a proffered plant for which I cannot visualize a place.

It is not my purpose to attempt a comprehensive work on color. Rather is it my intention to provide a starting point for those groping with color for the first time, by means of actual examples of pleasing combinations. I do not suggest that the echoes approach is the only way of coordinating garden color, nor even necessarily the best. I do think, however, that coordinated color makes a garden more romantic, and that the echoes concept is the easiest way to begin.

A recent letter in a gardening magazine asked why we must keep fussing about garden design, about color, about what goes with what. "Can't we just enjoy our gardens?" was its heartcry. Of course we can, of course we should, and of course we do, each of us picking from a smorgasbord of plants and following a chosen style or fashioning our own. I wholeheartedly endorse the sentiment of Friedrich Nietzsche, when he wrote: "This is *my* way, what is yours? As for *the* way, it does not exist."

I dedicate this book to the spirit of experiment, and to all of you who listen, consider, select, then march to your own drummer.

Echoes Defined,
the Fashion for Color, Massing

Put in a nutshell, a color echo is the repetition of color as a means of creating unity, serenity, interest, and charm in a garden. At first noticing only vignettes—those felicitous color partnerships where two plants are tied together by a common hue yet retain their individuality—I gradually became aware of the wider role that coordinated color plays in the gardens where I linger longest. In large gardens and small, with two plants or two hundred, color repetition helps bring about harmony and enables each plant to give its best.

The many kinds of echo include: highlighting the secondary color in a flower or leaf by putting it next to a plant of matching solid color; putting together plants with flowers of similar color but different size or shape; toning down a strongly colored plant with one of a paler tint, or doing the reverse to enliven a dull color; putting together two foliage plants of the same color but different form or texture; picking up the color of berries or autumn foliage in an underplanting; matching flower or foliage color to such structural or ornamental elements as fences, paths, or birdhouses; spacing the same plant, or different plants of similar shape and color, along a border to provide continuity; making beds and borders more cohesive and melodic by selecting one main hue as the connecting link. These will be discussed and illustrated later, but first a look at the subject of gardens in general and color in particular.

What do we ask of our gardens? Many plots seem at first glance solely functional: a lawn on which children can play, a silver maple (a poor choice but favored because it is fast growing) for shade, a patio for the cookout, perhaps a section for vegetables. But why the solitary crab apple or cherry, and why the bedded-out impatiens and marigolds if not for their color or beauty (where bedding plants are concerned, this is not, alas, always the same thing)? Most of us seek a measure of romance from our individual Edens.

Circumstances of place, and time, and means, and personality fashion the garden dream into its varied shapes. Classical gardens laid a foundation of geometric order, a restfulness of green hedges, gray stone, pellucid or fountain-dappled water, embellishing it with ornament, frequently grand, even grotesque, but skillfully crafted. Victorians added color to heavyweight formality, frequently in a manner now considered tasteless. The naturalistic school achieved its goal with unapparent artifice in the parkland approach of trees, grass, and gentle motion from imperturbable cud-chewing cows, or the more exotic herd of deer or elegant white swans. Cottagers and farmers' wives satisfied a need for beauty by incorporating flowers with the prosaic vegetables. Flower arrangers may want a cutting garden and those who pursue the gustatory arts herbs conveniently at hand in a dooryard garden. The adventurous and able find romance in wild places, and in inducing plants found there to grow in their gardens. At the other extreme, a few potted plants may bring joy to the housebound elderly, or dwellers in high-rise city apartments. The need for growing things is deeply ingrained in us, as is, recognized or not, the need for creative endeavor. Garden making is one of the creative arts and as such will be, and should be, expressed in individual and often experimental ways.

At any one time, however, some prevailing need or whim seems to be "in the wind," as it were, arising, it seems, as part of a checks-and-balances process in the pattern of our lives. At present there are two major movements. Concern that a burgeoning population threatens to destroy the natural world is causing many gardeners to eschew structure and strive to create settings for their homes less obviously shaped by human hands and needing less human intervention in the form of water or fertilizer. The increasing use of ornamental grasses and the attempts to rescue and reestablish endangered native plants are two elements of this. The dominant, and in some respects conflicting, craving, is, however, for color and romance, embodied in the resurgence of enthusiasm for perennials, a burgeoning interest in annuals that have not had the grace bred out of them, and a touch of nostalgia for "grandmother's flowers" and the fragrance of old-fashioned roses.

How might coordinated color help satisfy these desires and make our gardens more joyous places?

Through nearly forty years of garden making and garden visiting, I have heard, and voiced, two main criticisms of gardens at large. The first is that the garden is overstructured and underplanted. This may not call for change if all the owners want is a neat setting for the house and minimal maintenance, but guests aren't likely to take time to "smell the roses" on their way to the front door.

The reverse of this is the collector's garden, where dinner guests may linger so long discussing each plant that the food spoils. Plantsmanship combined with artistry results in lovely gardens (every one of the gardens about to be mentioned is owned or managed by a knowledgeable plantsperson) but when squeezing in the maximum number of plants is the sole criterion, the result is often uncohesive and restless. To plantspeople such a garden has its own magic, to others it is just a hodgepodge of plants and haphazard spots of color.

The challenge lies in achieving unity while still including sufficient different plants, pleasingly combined, to make the garden interesting. Rock gardens serve the collector well because the rocks form a connecting link and a soothing background color. The less structure there is in a garden, whether provided by rocks, paths, walls, or hedges clipped as structural elements, the greater the need for some unifying factor among the plants. In woodland gardens (the closest to natural that gardens get) trees fill this role, and any note of formality, whether of structure or planting, strikes the wrong note, but echoes still have a place. Viki Ferreniea, author of *Wildflowers in Your Garden,* writes: "Sometimes a plant's full potential is not realized until it is displayed in combination with other plants that highlight its true beauty." That is the essence of color echoes. In small gardens, or small groupings, it is particularly important to get the very best from every plant.

Whether a garden is overstructured and underplanted, or the reverse, coordinated color can go a long way toward redressing the balance, and at very little cost. It can make a structured garden more welcoming, and it can be a unifying factor in the plantsman's garden. Perhaps more important, it can be a tremendous source of creative satisfaction.

Homeowners want more romance and color in their

gardens and romantic gardens call for flowers, but flowers alone are not enough; they are too ephemeral, especially in hot climates, and therefore by nature a succession of bit players, in the main. We need to pay more attention to foliage as a garden's main cohesive factor, not as texture—a topic well covered in books and articles, but as color. It is in this context that I have chosen to place it, though the role of shape and texture is not overlooked. Analysis of the photographs will make plain the importance of foliage in this role, and that colorful gardens can, in fact, be made with foliage alone.

Any attempted analysis of what makes for a great garden of the romantic kind might well begin with visits to a few of international acclaim. In England these include two National Trust gardens, Sissinghurst and Tintinhull, and two privately owned gardens open to visitors, John Treasure's Burford House, near Tenbury Wells, and Lord and Lady Fitzwalter's Goodnestone Park, near Canterbury. All are on a grander scale than most of us can manage but all contain areas, or "rooms," no larger than the average suburban garden, and even some that would fit into a small city lot. All abound in ideas and combinations that could be emulated in small patches of ground. So does Christopher Lloyd's Great Dixter, in Sussex, and here the wild element has been introduced, with cow parsley (*Anthriscus sylvestris*), the English version of Queen Anne's lace, sweeping up to the walls and an orchard turned into meadow.

In the United States two gardens of which I never tire are Wave Hill, barely a stone's throw from New York City, which is open most days, and Frank Cabot's Stonecrop in Cold Spring, New York, which may be visited by appointment. Their flower gardens, presided over by Marco Polo Stufano and Caroline Burgess, respectively, are magical places, and imitable—in scale and structure if not in artistry— in many home gardens.

The Wild Garden at Wave Hill is of particular interest to those wanting a natural garden. It is not a garden for native plants, as the name first led me to suppose, though many native plants would be at home there, and it is far from wild in the sense of being left to its own devices; rather, plants are brought together, in balanced proportions and carefully considered colors, without formal structure or apparent artifice, large rocks providing the only "hardscaping."

What do such gardens of universal appeal have in common? To begin with, either time or money. Let us not pretend that money makes no difference: one component of most such gardens is beautiful structure, and this is very expensive. Note, however, that expensive structure is not an ingredient in the Wild Garden at Wave Hill. Dedication is more important, and abundant time spent working in a garden goes a long way toward compensating for a limited budget. When

Caryopteris × *clandonensis* 'Longwood Blue' is underplanted with *Sternbergia lutea,* an autumn-flowering bulb, in a composition that is simple, formal, and serene. (Longwood Gardens, Pennsylvania; September)

both time and money are in short supply, there is a problem, but those to whom gardening is important usually manage to plan their lives in a way that leaves sufficient time—if seldom as much as we might like—to devote to this passion.

Color (but never haphazard color) is a common denominator in these gardens, as is the successful balancing of two seemingly opposing factors, simplicity and intricacy. Simplicity, if overdone, fails to hold the attention of the viewer for more than a few minutes. This may sometimes be intentional—freeing the mind to drift into inner contemplation—but usually we seek more sustained interest from a garden. Intricacy, carried too far, is restless. These factors are intertwined with the way color is used, simplicity resulting from the use of a limited range within one area, intricacy from the individual plants and the way they are combined.

Simplicity can be achieved by the massing of a single plant. In the wild the most striking scenes often consist of just one kind of plant, growing in breathtaking profusion, but our reaction has much to do with the grandeur of the setting. Surround the same expanse of plants with buildings, reduce the scale, or clutter up the scene and the sense of awe is lost.

Massing, with appropriate choice of color, can be dramatic, and it involves less effort, and less thought, then weaving a tapestry of intermingled colors. Part of the drama is that such displays are usually of short duration. They can be prolonged by choosing a plant that will look good and continue to flower for a protracted period, but seen day after day such scenes quickly pall.

Massing is a mainstay of many public parks, where it works extremely well. The setting is usually spacious, most visits are brief or infrequent, and while the spring tulips are putting on a dazzling display, annuals to take their place are being grown on in greenhouses. If your garden is your plaything and the canvas on which you paint your pictures, massing will fail to satisfy, for it leaves little scope for artistry, lacks the almost daily changes that are both the joy and the

Those who despise red salvia would surely think again on seeing this river of red, rendered even more dramatic by its complementary color, green, at Leaming's Run, a showplace for annuals, many of them color coordinated. (Leaming's Run Gardens, Cape May, New Jersey; August)

despair of gardeners, and finds no place for stretching one's knowledge of plants by the acquisition of something new.

Massing is an extreme form of repetition. Each plant merges its identity into the whole. This has the virtue of simplicity at the cost of interest. Echoes call for repetition but also for contrast in color, form, or texture. Massed plantings and echoes are not, however, incompatible. Forget-me-nots, for example, are often used as underplanting for spring bulbs. Pink ones could echo tulips of a similar or brighter pink, and blue ones could echo hyacinths of a darker blue. White tulips or white hyacinths could be underplanted with white arabis or phlox. Such simple echoes are effective on any scale. Where a public garden might use five thousand tulips, fifty would do in a garden of medium size, and a handful or two in a very small one.

The opposite of massing is the color equivalent of the

9

collector's garden: a bit of this and a bit of that and let the colors fall where they may. Such color-strewn compositions often have a lilting gaiety, especially when there is uniformity of flower form, as in mixed color strains of such annuals as zinnias, and the color is offset by a cool and simple setting of lawn or paving. But the eye quickly tires of a cacophony of color, so this, like massing, is an approach better suited to public parks than to private gardens.

If a garden is to be varied, and ever-changing, the challenge is to assemble one's collection, or paint one's picture, in a melodious manner. This is most readily achieved by deciding upon an overall theme for each area, based on one major hue, then adding only those colors that harmonize with it. When plantings are complex but united by cadences of color, we have the best of two worlds: some of the simplicity of mass, and much of the interest of variety. Far from being limiting, it offers abundant scope for artist and plant collector

This complex combination is united by common colors, the scarlet, yellow, and orange recurring in the tulips 'Oriental Splendour' and 'Oxford's Elite' and in the underplanting of pansies. Though striking in overall effect, the detail might go unnoticed by most visitors viewing large-scale public plantings. In the home garden, where individual plants and small groupings are more closely observed and analyzed, the intricacy and artistry of the combination would be better appreciated. (Tryon Palace Restoration, New Bern, North Carolina; April)

alike. And it has the practical advantage of reducing the amount of time spent walking round and round the garden wondering where to place that newly acquired treasure. Gardens of average size have room for more than one bed, and when each has a color theme it is easier to see where a new plant fits into the scheme of things. I like both pink and scarlet, but not together, so each has its separate place.

It is possible to have different ranges of color within an area at different seasons but achieving this is one of gardening's more advanced techinques, calling for an extensive mental inventory of plants and when, and for how long, they bloom. Books help only to a limited degree because flowering times vary from one region to another, and not uniformly for all plants.

Color-coordinated gardens first invite attention with their overall effect, then reward it with small incidents deserving of closer inspection and analysis—pictures within the picture, complete in themselves yet part of the whole. One

The magenta flowers of *Silene armeria* are echoed in the softer hue and different form of *Allium* 'Forescate', a selected form of chives. (Jerry Sedenko, Seattle, Washington; Late June)

The three kinds of flower are all of a similar yellow but quite different in form. The goldenrod is *Solidago verna,* the daylily was grown from seed, the yellow daisies are the gray-leaved *Eriophyllum lanatum.* (Jerry Sedenko, Seattle, Washington; Late June)

small unit makes a good starting point for a bed or border. It is then rather like doing a jigsaw puzzle: with the first few pieces in place it becomes much easier to see where other pieces might fit. And when the piece isn't, after all, a perfect fit, replacing it doesn't involve reshuffling the whole puzzle.

Much of the emphasis in this book is on small units, grouped by color. Units within these color groupings could be linked into extended themes, with accents of contrasting color added when thought desirable. Alternatively, units from different color groupings could be spaced, like pools in a stream, among quieter colors.

Although it might seem that very small gardens call for more color restraint than large ones, that isn't necessarily so. What the eye takes in is affected by the angle of viewing. If the whole length of a border is viewed head-on—across a lawn, for instance—combative colors need to be a long way apart, which calls for a very long border. The head cannot,

however, turn two ways at once, and human eyes have limited side vision, so in small gardens there may be sufficient
visual separation when warring colors are placed on opposite
sides of a path, as the following picture demonstrates. Clash-
ing colors, or plants so similar in color and form that they
nullify each other, can also sometimes be sufficiently separated by a bench, container, or ornament.

Magenta and yellow aren't colors most gardeners dare put together but they were, in fact, placed quite close together in this very small town garden, rich in colors and combinations. The gray foliage is a harmonizing factor, and the path provides visual separation between two strong colors which would be less pleasing placed side by side. The picture was taken on a wide angle lens, which sees further to the sides than the human eye, which would tend to focus first on the seat terminating the path, then to seek out detail and become absorbed in individual groupings. Other plants include sweet alyssum (*Lobularia maritima*), gray woolly thyme (*Thymus pseudolanuginosus*), *Diascia vigilis, Lavatera* 'Barnsley', *Verbascum bombyciferum, Achillea* 'Moonshine', and the small, silver-leaved *Achillea* × *kellereri* (Jerry Sedenko, Seattle, Washington; Late June)

The Language of  Color 1

Color theory is more akin to mathematics than to art, and I doubt that artistry can be defined in scientific terms. Studying color has, nevertheless, broadened my perspective and laid a firmer foundation on which to base experiments. I knew the "how" of garden color, intuitively or from years of trial and error, but not always the "why?" What has taxed me most over the years is not the downright awful, which is rare and to some degree subjective, nor the exhilarating cymbal clash of strongly contrasting color, which has its place though it is easily overdone, but the melody gone ever so slightly off-key. In my garden this has usually resulted from failure to identify the precise relationship of a yellow with a yellow, a blue with a blue, and so on. All yellows don't "go" with all other yellows, nor all blues with all other blues, and so on—not, that is, in direct association. Pure red, yellow, and blue form dividing lines and it is important to recognize on which side of that line other reds and pinks, yellows, or blues and purples fall. They are not split evenly;

A hot-color border with *Kerria japonica* 'Pleniflora', *Aquilegia canadensis,* tulip 'Queen of Sheba', *Euonymus* 'Sparkle 'n' Gold'. These colors, though hot, are also harmonious. (My garden; April)

15

there are, for instance, far more blues containing red than blues containing yellow. This becomes apparent on a color chart.

The other thing brought home to me from poring over color charts was that colors thought incompatible can be brought together if taken one tiny color step at a time. Take orange and pink, a combination disliked by nearly everyone, supporting the tenet that red containing blue (which most pinks do) should not be mixed with red containing yellow. From orange to pink is quite a big jump across the color spectrum, twelve steps, let's say, for purposes of comparison (colors can be changed in infinitessimal increments, so it could as well be twenty, or two hundred). Midway between them is red. On one side of this is a red-scarlet containing the merest hint of yellow. On the other side is red-crimson containing minimal blue. These three colors don't fight, where a bluer crimson might with a yellower scarlet—three steps, not twelve. It needs a fairly expansive border, however, if colors are to merge in this step-by-step way.

From this it can be inferred that, for reasons of space, if a full range of related colors is to be used in a melodic color scheme, some colors will have to be excluded. Echo themes don't use fewer colors, they may use more, but all fall within a limited part of the spectrum. If asked for simple ground rules for coordinating color, I'd suggest these:

1. Recognize the importance of "blender colors" (defined later), especially the foliage colors of green, gray, purple, chartreuse, and cream in the form of variegated foliage, and use them in generous quantity;

2. Work with a limited range of harmonious colors, making a favorite color, or combination of colors (blue and yellow, or pink and blue, for instance), your leitmotif and expanding the theme around them with closely related tones, tints, and shades;

3. Recognize where each primary is split (does a blue, for instance, fall on the violet-red side of pure blue, or on

the green–yellow side), then stay on one side or the other.

It is these suggestions that my color echoes theme embraces.

Color is, in a way, an illusion. What we see is the effect of light waves of varying lengths on the retina of the human eye. Black is the absence of color. True black cannot reflect light. There are no black flowers. Those that appear so are very dark shades of violet or purple: the violas 'Bowles' Black' and 'Molly Sanderson' are two such flowers. White is the opposite. Though often thought of as lacking color, it actually contains all the rays of the spectrum visible to the human eye and as such is, when pure, a very bright color.

Many animals and insects see things differently from us, being "blind" to some colors we can see, or able to see colors that are invisible to our eyes. It is possible that all human beings do not see color in precisely the same way but the surprising uniformity of color preferences across sex, age, and racial lines suggests that apparent differences probably come from our poor color vocabulary: what we see is the same color, we just have different names for it. This makes it extremely difficult to describe colors in a way helpful to all.

Language is not static, it develops and changes to meet the needs of a culture: when airplanes and automobiles were invented, words to describe them had to be created. The language of color is often inadequate or confusing, especially when we try to relate it to flowers. Writers of books and catalogues are frequently criticized for penning (typewriting! computerwriting!) misleading color descriptions. It is not for want of trying, but often we are literally at a loss for words to convey precisely what we mean. While color is obviously not new, it has not been a topic of sufficiently widespread interest within the gardening world to generate a broad range of definitive color descriptions, or even indeed to bring into general use words that do exist: a large proportion of words in the dictionary lie dormant most of the time. In George

Schmid's scholarly book *The Genus Hosta* I was pleased to see three words pulled out of obscurity—viridiscence (greenish), lutescence (yellowish), and albescence (whitish)—to describe a phenomenon common in hybrid hostas, the way many hosta leaves, or parts of them, become greener, yellower, or whiter as the season progresses. So efforts are being made, but a good deal of vagueness will inevitably remain because the mind's capacity to store precise color images seems to be limited.

In 1941 the Royal Horticultural Society published its Horticultural Color Chart. In order to describe the colors of plants in a uniform and recognizable way, it gave each color a name. The stated hope was that these names would "provide some mental picture of the colour and become widely used." That hope was not realized, for reasons noted in the introduction to the revised chart published in 1966: "The very multiplicity of colour names defeated its own object; colour memory is rarely good enough to remember what a named colour is like, while some names are meaningless to the great majority of people." What, for example, do these color chart descriptions convey to you: Naples yellow, aureolin, Orient pink, chrysocolla green?

The revised color chart published in 1966 relied on numbers to identify the colors, but numbers are helpful only to the few who own the chart. The numbers were cross-referenced to names used in the earlier chart, and also to names and numbers used in some other color references. That the lemon yellow of one chart becomes straw in another and aconite yellow in a third, while majolica yellow becomes apricot, and jasper red becomes begonia, adds to the confusion.

So in trying to describe color we walk on quaking ground. Few gardeners have the time or inclination to study such technical color-defining techniques as those established by the Commission Internationale de l'Eclairage, in which (quoting again from the explanatory pamphlet with the RHS Color Chart) "a colour could be specified by its co-ordinates (x,y) on the chromaticity chart (a form of colour triangle) and by Y, which is a measure of the percentage reflection of the sample."

At the simplest level, descriptions matched to familiar objects convey a rough idea of what one has in mind: lemon yellow, apricot, grass green, or brick red, for example. But can you distinguish between marigold and carrot? Glancing through the first catalogue to come to hand, I find such color descriptions as "campanula blue" and "rose pink." Which campanula? Which rose? Some of us perceive rose pink, or rosy pink as a warm pink, touched with yellow, others think of it as a cool pink, containing blue.

In her book *Still Life,* A.S. Byatt muses on this problem: "How would one find the exact word for the color of the plumskins. . . . There was a problem of accurate notation, which was partly a problem of sufficiency of adjectives. Do we have enough words, synonyms, near synonyms for purple? What *is* the grayish, or maybe white, or whitish, or silvery, or dusty mist or haze or smokiness over the purple shine? How do you describe the dark cleft from stalk pit to oval end, its inky shadow? . . . A writer aiming for unadorned immediacy might say a plum, a pear, an apple, and by naming these things evoke in every reader's mind a different plum, a dull tomato-and-green specked Victoria, a yellow-buff globular plum, a tight, black-purple damson. If he wishes to share a vision of a specific plum he must exclude and evoke: a matte, oval, purple-black plum, with a pronounced cleft."

The elusiveness of meaningful color descriptions was brought home to me while taking the picture on page 84. What color is the barn? "Brown," you'll probably say, yet it is the same color as the barberries we call purple. Such vagueness, though unavoidable, results in many disappointments when a plant turns out to be a different color from what was expected: the success of garden centers is due in part to buyers being able to see exactly what they are getting.

The dictionary may or may not clarify what is meant.

Mauve, lilac, and lavender are color terms frequently used. My dictionary defines them all as "pale purple." In the broad sense, so they are, but dozens of colors could be so described. "Lilac" and "lavender" are used to distinguish between pale purples containing different amounts of pink, lilac being pinker than lavender, but there's a middle point where either would be equally appropriate—or inappropriate. When flower names are used to describe a color they usually refer to the color of species or old-fashioned kinds: lavenders grown in today's gardens are more likely to be purple or violet-blue than the color to which they have lent their name, so this color term might well cause young gardeners to conjure up an image different from that intended.

Now that so many gardening books are profusely illustrated, pictures help, but the eye is more sensitive than the camera to subtleties of color. One regrettable consequence is that some of the dreamiest scenes and combinations never appear in books because their subtleties cannot be adequately captured on film. In this category came a delicate late-summer combination photographed at Wave Hill, where clumps of *Scilla scilloides,* a little bulb with flowers of palest pastel purple, emerged through a carpet of creeping thyme of similar soft color. No film renders all colors absolutely true, and a photograph taken in bright sunshine will render colors somewhat differently from the same scene photographed on an overcast day. Regardless of the weather, the time of day also influences color, both to the eye and to the color film.

Colors can be adjusted during the printing process, but it is unrealistic to expect technicians and picture editors to know the exact color of every plant. In reality, colors often become even more skewed in the course of reproduction. Even when the color is faithfully reproduced, something is missing: when light is beamed through a projected color slide, the glow of living flowers is there, but much of this is lost on the printed page.

Color Theory, Color Wheels

In painterly terms, the primary colors are red, yellow, and blue. All other colors are mixtures of two or more of these. Mixing all three together produces brown. (Brown is usually a better color than green for rendering garden stakes inconspicuous and one English gardening writer used to suggest mixing leftover oddments of paint from sundry projects to produce a suitable brown. My advice is that you buy the basic rusty brown "Rustoleum" undercoating paint for this purpose.)

Form the primary colors into a triangle, mix adjacent colors together in equal quantity, and we get the secondary colors of orange, green, and violet. We now have the spectral colors, as seen in a rainbow: red, orange, yellow, green, blue, and violet. These are pure, or *saturated,* colors. For convenience in formulating color theory, the six primary and sec-

An echo combination in the hot-color border, with the yellow edge to the tulip petals repeating the chartreuse-yellow of the euonymus.

ondary colors are formed into a circle to form the color wheel. There is more than one color wheel but this is the commonest.

The first three colors, red, orange, and yellow, are considered "hot" colors (lemon yellows are not, however, hot). In the garden hot colors seem nearer than they actually are. The other three colors, green, blue, and violet, are considered "cool." The cool colors, especially violet, seem further away than they are.

The language of color theory is seldom strictly adhered to, if at all, in gardening books and magazines, where the same words usually carry less closely defined, and sometimes quite different, meanings. The following brief discussion defines, in simplified form, some of the words basic to color theory and the color wheel.

Color is the broad term that covers everything. *Hue* defines it more narrowly: a red, a blue, a green, etc. Flowers of a pure, saturated hue are fairly few and this is just as well: clear, saturated hues are intense, brilliant colors and a little is usually better than a lot. Examples are *Crocosmia* 'Lucifer' (red), *Pulmonaria angustifolia* (pure blue when open, though pink in bud), and the sundrops usually sold as *Oenothera fruticosa*—some taxonomists dispute the correctness of the name—(yellow). Most colors are the less intense tones, tints, or shades. *Tone* describes a modified color, a hue to which another color has been added. Add white to a color and we get a *tint*. Add black and we get a *shade*. If sufficient white is added to make a color pale and delicate, it is a *pastel*.

Brightness, value, and *luminosity* define the light-reflecting quality of a color. Yellow is the brightest color in the spectrum, violet the least bright. Bright colors stand out among duller ones. The apparent brightness of a color is influenced by its neighbors. White, for instance, intensifies adjacent colors, making it a poor choice for separating two that clash.

When gardeners speak of harmonious colors they usually mean any combination of two or more colors that is pleasing to the eye. It is in this broad sense that I use the term in this book. The opposite phenomenon is the color clash that occurs

when combinations strike a jarring note. In color wheel terminology the definition is much narrower, *harmonizing* colors being those next to each other on the color wheel and having a pigment in common: red with orange (orange contains red), orange with yellow (orange contains yellow), yellow with green (green contains yellow), and so on through green with blue, blue with violet, and violet with red.

Interpretations of *contrasting* colors also vary. In the narrowest sense, contrasts share no pigment: red and yellow; yellow and blue; blue and red. The dictionary definition supports this with "the opposition or dissimilarity by which one heightens the effect of the other." Gardeners apply the word more broadly, frequently meaning no more than that two

In this border yellow, the brightest color in the spectrum, is combined with luminous white. Yellow flag irises (*Iris pseudacorus*) are echoed by the lower-growing sundrops (*Oenothera tetragona riparia*), and the white in the miscanthus leaves is repeated by *Verbena tenuisecta* 'Alba' in the foreground. Other plants in the picture include gray-leaved, white-flowered *Lychnis coronaria* 'Alba' and a glaucous-bladed ornamental grass, *Panicum virgatum* 'Heavy Metal', which will form an architectural, upright clump about six feet high when fully grown. (North Carolina State University Arboretum, Raleigh)

colors are noticeably different: pale lavender and purple, for example.

When we come to *complementary* colors, confusion really reigns, largely because of its similarity to "complimentary," a word with the same Latin root but a different meaning. The former word is frequently used when the latter is intended: that is, any two colors that enhance or flatter each other. To complement means to complete, and the scientific definition of complementary color in my dictionary is "any two colors of the spectrum that combine to form white or whitish light: if a disk colored half yellow and half blue is rotated rapidly, it looks white or gray." Using this definition, blue and yellow are complementary colors. In color wheel terms, however, complementary colors are those opposite each other on the color wheel: red and green; yellow and violet; blue and orange. Put another way, complementary pairs consist of one primary color plus a secondary color made up of the other two primaries: red and green (green being a mixture of yellow and blue); yellow and violet (violet being a mixture of red and blue), or blue and orange (orange being a mixture of red and yellow). All three primary colors are therefore present. Because use of this word is more likely to obfuscate than to clarify, I try to avoid it except in the context of color theory.

Complementary colors and contrasting colors sound as if they'd be opposites, but in fact complementary colors (which share no pigment) are also contrasting colors, very strongly contrasting in fact. Not everyone would agree that complementary colors are always complimentary, they contrast too strongly for some tastes.

The main shortcoming of the color wheel, in its simple form, is that it deals only with spectral hues. Once we add the tones, tints, and shades that make up most of the gardener's palette, color wheel theory isn't very helpful. Crimson and scarlet share a pigment (red) but they are not usually considered harmonious neighbors. Nor, however, are they contrasting colors (colors sharing no pigment). There are few violet flowers, and still fewer red ones, compared with the plenitude of pink, but pink, the most popular garden color, has no place as such on the color wheel, nor do two of the garden's basic colors, the foliage colors of gray and purple. It takes a very mathematical mind to translate theory based only on spectral hues into the reality of the garden's myriad colors.

Although the RHS Color Chart doesn't give much guidance to the writer trying to define color in words, as a gardener I commend it as of immense practical value. The latest version can be bought from RHS Enterprises Ltd., RHS Garden, Wisley, Woking, Surrey GU23 6QB, England. The colors are presented in spectral order in four fans, with a fifth fan for dull "grayed" colors. As an example of the breadth of the color range, there are four different whites in this fan as well as four grayed whites, four greenish whites, four yellowish whites, and four orangish whites. Each leaf of a fan contains four patches, arranged in progressively paling tints: from red to pastel pink, for example. There are two hundred leaves, any one of which can be brought into juxtaposition with any other. One can therefore get an idea of how any two or more colors would look together, and how a color appears to change when adjacent colors are changed.

Spread out the four main fans (excluding grayed colors) into a circle and you get a giant color wheel with numerous gradations beween the main spectral hues. Pure green, for instance, is on the center leaf of one fan, with adjacent leaves showing increasing additions of yellow in one direction, and of blue in the other.

That colors are harmonious when they progress in spectral order becomes apparent. What also becomes apparent is that moving in orderly increments through the many hues would require an immense amount of garden space. The color echoes approach is to limit the number of primary and secondary colors, sometimes even to one, but to make full use of the many tones, tints, and shades within that range. It is important to recognize on which side of the primary hue a

The gentle combination of pinks, mauves, and whites preferred by many gardeners. Plants include foxgloves, *Geranium endressii,* bearded iris 'Irma Jones', *Oenothera speciosa,* the early Shasta daisy (*Chrysanthemum leucanthemum* 'May Queen'), a wallflower (*Erysimum* 'Bowles' Mauve'), and *Indigofera kirilowii.* (The Elizabeth Lawrence Border, North Carolina State University Arboretum, Raleigh; Design by Edith Eddleman and Douglas Ruhren)

color falls. It will mix well with adjacent colors on that side, but not always with those on the other side. Harmonious colors on the scarlet side of red are orange and the warmer yellows. On the cooler, crimson side, come the magentas, purples, lavenders, lilacs, and nearly all the pinks. Pure yellow may be out of place among the warm yellows and scarlets and mixes better with the lemony yellows on its cooler side, these in turn merging with greeny blues. On the other side of pure blue, colors become touched with pink, merging into violets, purples, and pinks.

The chart's limitation is that the colors, though numerous, are solid and, save as affected by colors placed next to them, unchanging. The explanatory notes with my 1966 chart

state: "Standard viewing conditions were maintained with an illumination of 100–200 lm/ft. sq., a neutral background of reflectance factor 15, B.S. 9–097 and freedom from glare and other extraneous factors likely to affect the visual response."

How different this is from plants in a garden setting. Few flowers contain only one color, and most are more luminous than the paint of color swatches. Pointillist painters developed a method of achieving more luminous color by laying tiny dots of color on a white background. When seen from a little way off the colors blend together into an apparent color different from any of its components. Monet achieved a similar effect at Giverny, where flowers of many kinds and colors are grown in strips, separated by narrow paths. Seen from outside the grid, the paths disappear and the effect is hazily, dreamily impressionistic. Individual plants and groupings come into focus only when you walk the paths. Unless trained to a more analytic approach, the eye does tend to blend the several colors often contained within a flower into an overall impression. When a garden lacks the space for impressionistic drifts, it becomes more important to get the very best it can give from every component in the picture, and to do this we need to pay closer attention to a plant's actual color or colors.

In the garden colors appear more intense under an overcast sky than they do in brilliant sunshine. This has shaped the preference for soft colors in cloudy regions. Gradually, American gardeners are learning that stronger colors may be needed to hold their own with the sun where blue skies and high summer temperatures are the norm. Nature has set the pattern: most red and orange flowers, like the hummingbirds drawn to them, come from warm regions. Many are killed by frost, so where summers are hot but winters cold, gardeners must rely mainly on annuals, or perennials treated as annuals (many red-flowered salvias, for instance) for these colors.

Within each garden, the light is constantly changing, varying with season, time of day, sun or shade, and the current weather pattern. Soil can also affect color: hydrangeas are a good example of this, many being blue in acid soil but pink when the soil is alkaline. Flower color also changes in the course of the natural progression from bud to fading bloom. The color of some flowers is strongest when the flower is newly opened, paling with maturity, with others the reverse. One of the targets of rose breeders has been red roses that hold their color until the petals drop. Many of the older ones turn a dingy color as they fade. The undersides of plant petals are often a different color from the surface, effecting a marked color change from bud to opened flower. Seed heads and fall leaf color may introduce further color notes.

So, despite the best efforts of color theorists, in the end the game has to be played out in the garden, relying on one's own judgment and preferences and doing a good deal of shifting around until one gets it right, or acceptably so. Mistakes get fewer with experience but never entirely cease. There are times when, for practical reasons, one settles for an aesthetic "good enough." I do not usually (there are always exceptions) enjoy purple and blue together. I don't find such combinations objectionable, they just aren't among those that hold me enthralled. In an east-facing border, however, a large and ever-spreading mass of *Campanula poscharskyana* is only three feet away from a sizable patch of the purple-flowered hardy orchid *Bletilla striata*. Both are well-established, healthy, undemanding, and able to contend with the roots of the pines under which they grow. And so I am content to prevent them from actually intermingling by positioning a large clump of variegated Solomon's seal (*Polygonatum odoratum* 'Variegatum') between them.

Choosing plants is no different from choosing clothes. Some have more flair than others but everyone knows what colors and combinations they like or dislike. Mistakes occur for the same reasons: impulse buys that don't fit into the scheme of things and leave one searching in vain along a rail of blouses to find one that goes with the new skirt. If one starts with a favorite color, then stays within a coordinated theme, the result is usually better, at lesser cost.

There's probably no mixture of colors that hasn't been tried by someone, somewhere, and exciting gardens frequently include unorthodox combinations. Whether we admire these, or flinch, they expand our color horizons and that is no bad thing. For crowd pleasers, or those lacking color confidence, certain combinations have emerged that nearly everybody likes. The most popular garden color scheme is composed of blues, pinks, grays, and whites, with or without the addition of smaller amounts of pale or lemon yellows. The reverse is also well liked: blues and yellows predominating, with touches of pastel pinks. A smaller but growing number of gardeners enjoy the hot colors of scarlet, orange, and golden yellow. Few want bright pink with bright yellow and fewer still tolerate bright pink and orange.

Combining colors is greatly facilitated when additions can be selected from plants in bloom. It is no coincidence that many of the most beautiful gardens are created by those connected with nurseries. I watched one designer at work, selecting from a truckload of plants in large containers, arranging and rearranging them on the ground, observing them at different times of day, adjusting proportions and making substitutions. Only when satisfied with the "mock up" was the combination transferred to his own or a client's garden, and even then with the expectation that further changes might be needed in a different setting.

Home gardeners can't do this but many can find space for a nursery bed or holding area, where plant acquisitions can be grown until it becomes clear where their color, shape, and blooming time best fit into the scheme of things. Blooms can then be picked and carried around for purposes of comparison. This way you'll know for sure that blooming times coincide—most years, anyway. It is a common misconception that flowering times remain synchronized, with plants blooming earlier, or later, some seasons but still together. Not so. Quite horrible combinations can occur when two

Above
The most popular color scheme is based on blue, pink, and white. Plants in this mixed border include *Spiraea nipponica* 'Snowmound', *Baptisia minor, Geranium endressii* 'A. T. Johnson', *Lonicera heckrottii, Iris sibirica, Verbena* 'Silver Anne', and coralbells (*Heuchera*). (My garden; May)

Opposite page
A pink and white spring echo combination in the above border. The pink of tulip 'New Design' echoes *Phlox subulata* 'Scarlet Flame', while the white edge to the tulip leaves is picked up by the white flowers of *Cornus florida* in the background and a white-striped yucca growing nearby. (My garden; April)

plants bloom together that usually would not. Don't rush to move one or the other, it is better to turn a blind eye to occasional discord caused by abnormal weather patterns, or to resolve the immediate problem by removing the blooms from one or more of the offending plants.

I find early morning walks in the garden conducive to cogitation, so this is the time when many a plant gets scheduled for a move. I've learned, though, not to do this immediately—and not only because I'm often still wearing a nightdress! What seems, in the misty early morning, to be the perfect spot for a plant often turns out to be less than ideal reassessed at high noon. When possible I grow my plants-in-waiting in sunken containers of generous size, with room for the roots to expand. It is always wise to do this with plants intolerant of root disturbance, gas plant (*Dictamnus*), for example. I use standard black plastic nursery containers, avoiding like the plague the kind with a slightly rolled-in rim, it

being impossible to knock a plant smoothly out of these with the soil ball intact. When a likely spot is found, the plant, still in its container, is plunged there for further evaluation—which may take a day or a season. If the time span is long enough for its roots to have filled the container (usually easy to ascertain by lifting it and looking to see if roots are emerging through the drainage holes) the plant is repotted before it is replunged.

Often a plant goes on trial in several places before the best place is found. If it is then high summer, I may, depending on the vulnerability of the plant, await a better planting time. With plants disliking disturbance the bottom is then cut out of the container (easily done with scissors), taking care that the soil does not fall out. The plant and bottomless container are then positioned in the prepared hole and the soil filled in, then the rest of the container is eased out unless it is a plant likely to be destroyed by voles (hostas and lilies in particular), in which case I may leave the bottomless container in place as a protective barrier.

This may seem to be a rather drawn-out procedure but it saves a good deal of subsequent shifting around when things don't work out as expected. An example of a color change effected by light occurred recently in my garden. In a hot color section I had planted a group of 'Girard's Hot Shot' evergreen azaleas in a shaded corner under a small dogwood, where sun was blocked from the south and west. Their color, a deep, glowing scarlet, was exactly right and the flowers long-lasting. I'd bought six but needed only five. At the other end of this section, some twenty feet away, a bare patch needed filling. Surveying this on an overcast day, it seemed to call for a balancing splash of scarlet and the surplus azalea seemed just the plant for the job. It was not: the dogwood didn't cast its shadow this far and hot sun flooding in from the south caused the flowers to fade fast. Worse, they took on pinkish tones quite wrong in this context.

A plant usually seen lit from the front will appear a different color when viewed from the other side. It will also have a different backdrop of colors. Gardens are occasionally designed to be walked around in only one direction: public gardens may have arrows pointing the way and visitors who attempt to swim against the tide are not popular. In many home gardens the route one takes varies. Reversing direction throws colors into a new light, both figuratively and literally: colors that don't impinge on each other when viewed from one side may do so when walking the other way. When space permits (very small gardens don't lend themselves to the meandering path approach), curving paths are better than straight ones because shrubs can be positioned at bends to block the view of what lies beyond, adding a touch of mystery as well as keeping colors apart.

Finding exactly the color one wants can't always be accomplished at a nursery. Most color-conscious gardeners maintain their own stock of some plants of a particularly desirable color, especially annuals, by collecting seed when they know this to come true, or by rooting cuttings to be wintered in frost-free frames, greenhouses, or indoor light units. Selected forms of sweet william (*Dianthus barbatus*), usually sold in mixed color strains, are one example. One I keep going with cuttings is a clear bright red, and another that comes true from seed has flowers of a plum purple so dark as to seem black. From time to time one forgets, or simply isn't there, to collect seed or take cuttings. The only resource then is to beg them back from the friends with whom, if one is wise as well as generous, they were earlier shared.

The eyes and leaves of yellow feverfew (*Chrysanthemum parthenium* 'Aureum') are repeated in the yellow petals of the gloriosa daisies, with contrast provided by the darker tones and the size of the flowers. (Kathryn McHolm, Ontario, Canada; July)

Exploring Echoes

2

Nuances of color often pass unnoticed: the very narrow, contrasting edge of a leaf, for instance, or petals suffused with more than one hue or tipped with contrasting color. "Bee guide" paths to the pollen might take the form of splotches or dots, as in foxgloves, or lines of color that bring to mind the outpatient department of our local hospital, where one follows a blue line to the X-ray department, a yellow one to the exit.

When describing a flower color we might say that it is pink, blue, or scarlet, when in fact it has a yellow eye, something so common among flowers that we take it for granted and tend not to see it. These yellow eyes become more pronounced against a background of yellow flowers or foliage. Yellow barberries make a good background and there's a recent addition to the popular *Berberis thunbergii* 'Aurea' in *B. t.* 'Bonanza Gold', a dense, compact, bright gold mounding form introduced by the wholesale Lake County Nursery in Ohio after extensive field testing to find a golden barberry that did not burn when grown in full sun. This was just what I needed as backdrop for the yellow-rimmed scarlet flowers of *Gaillardia* 'Goblin'.

White narcissus with yellow cups provide fine opportunities for double echoes. In my garden *Narcissus* 'Martha Washington' pops up each spring through an evergreen mat of *Arabis procurrens* in front of the old-fashioned, reliable, double-flowered *Kerria japonica* 'Pleniflora'. The cup of the narcissus matches the yellow of the kerria flowers while its perianth (petals) matches the white of the arabis.

Other flowers have dark eyes: the delicate, pale yellow annual *Hibiscus trionum* is one of them, and at Wave Hill I saw it combined with purple basil to accentuate its dusky eye. Sometimes a contrasting eye is only noticeable under certain light conditions—one of the rewards of walking around one's garden often and at different hours. The disk flowers of *Gaillardia* 'Burgundy' form a dome of darker, denser purple than the petals or ray florets. When backlit or sidelit the disk stands out in dark relief against petals a glowing wine red. In the border designed by Edith Eddleman and Doug Ruhren at North Carolina State University this gaillardia was set against the bold leaves of a purple canna.

Thinking "echoes" makes one more aware of color variations and therefore better able to position plants and give them companions that make elusive qualities more evident— to notice, for instance, that the slender tubular flowers of *Phygelius* 'African Queen' have citron yellow throats within their burgundy-colored mouths. The flowers hang shyly down and only when I was on my knees weeding did I get a glimpse inside the flowers. Growing it in a raised bed with an underplanting of golden thyme to create an emphasizing echo wins more admiration for it.

Delicate though they are, there's no need to get on hands and knees to pay homage to gray-leaved *Lychnis coronaria* 'Oculata' ('Angel Blush' is a prettier name but it seems to be the same plant), a short-lived, self-sowing plant that never looks out of place no matter where it appears, in sun or shade.

The cerise-eyed white flowers face obligingly upward for easy inspection. They benefit, nevertheless, from association with flowers of brighter or denser pink. Try it behind a group of the low-growing, bright pink *Phlox amoena* or the bushy little *Spiraea japonica* 'Alpina', or use it to gentle down the magenta spires of purple loosestrife (*Lythrum salicaria*) if state regulations do not prohibit growing this where you live. It also makes a perfect companion for such deep pink old-fashioned roses as 'Cardinal de Richelieu' or 'William Lobb', or such "new old-fashioned" English roses as 'Othello'. (*Roses,* by Roger Phillips and Martyn Rix, is a book I like to have on hand for checking the colors of roses. It contains over fourteen hundred color photographs and the colors are portrayed with exceptional accuracy.)

Lamb's ears (*Stachys byzantina*) is a well-loved and widely grown foliage plant. Its flowers seldom draw admiring comment and the nonflowering form, 'Silver Carpet', is frequently preferred. I've seen the flowers described as dingy, but all they need is a little help. Put lamb's ears in front of *Malva moschata* and its spikes of tiny flowers—magenta but with the appearance of pale pink because they are swathed in gray velvety calyces—have a better chance of being appreciated, for themselves and for their contrast in size and form with the silver-pink flower saucers of the mallow. *Gaura lindheimeri,* on the other hand, is noteworthy for its cloud of small white flowers, borne in continuing display through summer into autumn. Have you noticed that each flower is faintly blushing, the pink becoming more pronounced as the flowers fade? Attention is drawn to this when the flowers of *Clematis* 'Hagley Hybrid', soft pink but large, ramble among its stems or climb a nearby support. By autumn gaura's willowy stems have turned deep pink and I then plug in a chrysanthemum of matching color, clearing space for this if necessary by pulling out annuals that begin to look decrepit.

Dainty *Calamintha nepeta* adds airy grace to any planting. Seed strains vary in color, from white through pale pink or lavender to blue, and some have larger flowers than others.

The delicate combinations of colors present in many irises make them candidates for beautiful, if fleeting, echoes. Here a sisyrinchium picks up the coloring in the falls of a Pacific hybrid iris. (Harland Hand, California; May)

The one fittingly called 'White Cloud' makes a beautiful echo with the stiff leaf swords of the white-striped *Iris pallida* 'Argentea Variegata'. The similar *Calamintha sylvatica* (the better choice for a shady spot) also varies from pink to lavender to blue. When you have a color you particularly like, it is easily increased from cuttings.

Forgive me if I try to describe an exquisite combination in the border at the North Carolina State University without precisely identifying one plant in the partnership. It was grown from seed labeled *Potentilla nepalensis* 'Miss Willmott', but Miss Willmott would have spurned it as a changeling, her true child—rarely available—being cherry pink. This one was more nearly scarlet and coral, touched with crimson at the eye, pastel at the rim, a symphony of color in its own

right and lovelier still augmented by *Stachys coccinea,* a tender plant from Mexico with short spires of softly scarlet tubular flowers. Among potentilla cultivars known to me, 'Roxana' is the nearest to what I saw.

A quick survey of my own garden in June showed that less than half the flowers I grow are a solid color. A second color, and sometimes a third, may occur in the throat, heart, or petal tip of a flower, and once one starts to pay attention, echo potential is found in a plethora of stripes, streaks, splashes, feathering, and picotee patterning, subtle or pronounced. Any such flower can be the nucleus for cadences of matching color in the surrounding plants.

The keynote for one such grouping in my garden is the yellow bee guides on the falls of a violet-purple Japanese iris.

Varying tints and shades of the same color always create pleasing echoes and *Primula sieboldii* makes an appropriate underplanting for the strap-petaled azalea 'Koromo Shikibu'. (My garden; May)

The yellow "bee guides" on the petals of a Japanese iris grown from seed are given emphasis by the accompanying yellow of *Hemerocallis* 'Mme. Bellum' and verbascum. (My garden; Early June)

This is echoed by the yellow of my favorite daylily, 'Mme. Bellum'. I know no nursery source for this, but *Hemerocallis* 'Corky' flowers at the same time and seems to differ only in being a bit shorter. The yellow is repeated again in the eight-foot-high candelabrum of a self-sown verbascum and once more, by intent, in *Althaea ficifolia* (syn. *A. rugosa*), an exquisite hollyhock with single flowers of pale lemon yellow, deepening in the center. It is not long-lived but it self sows and the seedlings are true to color provided there are no other hollyhocks nearby with which it might fraternize.

One learns that it does no good to dream beautiful dreams if the plants of one's choice make it plain that where they've been put is not where they want to be, or if one or the other stages a takeover bid. Sometimes a good deal of thought is needed, and repeated experiment, before one either gets it right or gives up trying. So it was in my garden with two forms of *Symphytum grandiflorum* called 'Hidcote Blue' and 'Hidcote Pink'. Their names are an exaggeration, the nodding tubular flowers being primarily cream, with a minimal amount of blue or pink at the top of the tube, though it is at least on the outside of the tube, and fairly pronounced in the shepherd's-crook clusters of congested buds. They flower in spring, when there are lots of blue flowers, so finding a suitable companion for 'Hidcote Blue' shouldn't have been difficult. Comfreys, however, are dense and vigorous plants that frequently smother out their neighbors. Faced with such tough competition, many a plant would quietly disappear before the gardener realized what was happening, but Spanish bluebells (*Scilla hispanica* of most catalogues, *Hyacinthoides hispanica* in more erudite publications) have proved able to hold their own. These invincible plants raise their sturdy stems of flared blue bells above the comfrey, which later hides their withering leaves. So far they've needed no help from me but I do halt the spread of the comfrey during those hours devoted to search-and-rescue missions in the garden. It isn't always easy to find time for this, when other tasks seem more pressing, but is an important aspect of gardening if some cherished plants are not to disappear for good.

It took me a couple of seasons to find suitable companions for *Symphytum* 'Hidcote Pink' which has coral-colored buds—not the easiest color to match. It now laps the ankles of that scourge of the south (some think), *Photinia* × *fraseri,* a large evergreen shrub with coppery new leaves quite well matched to the coral of the comfrey. By the time the comfrey has had its fling, the apricot pink flowers of *Rosa* 'Cornelia' are creating another echo with the photinia foliage. 'Cornelia' isn't supposed to be a climbing rose but in the heat and moisture of coastal Virginia, climb it does. Perhaps "loll" would be a better word for the long, lax canes, and considering that the temperature may now be climbing into the nineties, who can blame it?

Echo potential isn't only found in flowers. Stem color, the flush of pink or purple characteristic of much new growth, leaf veining, fruits, and bark can all play a part. I'd never noticed the pink tint to the stems and veining of *Euphorbia sikkimensis* until I saw it combined with pink lilies in Eleanor Carnwath's Seattle garden. The 'Peacock' ornamental kales have contrasting veining in their prettily cut and curled gray-green leaves. In 'White Peacock' the contrast is pronounced. The purplish pink veining in 'Pink Peacock' is less immediately obvious and needs accentuating by association with something of more pronounced purple. For long-lasting effect I'd suggest purple globe amaranth (*Gomphrena globosa*), which carries its bobbles of bloom all through the growing season.

Sedum 'Weihenstephaner Gold', an excellent carpeter for the front of a border and still better displayed at the edge of a raised bed, bears its starry flowers in such profusion that it becomes a solid, unmissable patch of yellow, but how many, I wonder, notice the starry red seed capsules that follow? They

This combination in my garden came about partly by chance. The pinkish selection of *Calamintha nepeta* echoes the pale pink of the fully opened chrysanthemum flowers, while the deeper pink of *Poliomintha nepeta,* just visible bottom right, matches the chrysanthemum's buds and newly opened flowers. The chrysanthemum was a self-sown seedling, its color not known when the other two plants, raised from seed and cuttings respectively, were used to fill empty spaces in a bed with a pink theme.

are nicely timed to coincide with the two-tone crimson flowers of *Potentilla thurberi*.

Having noticed that a proportion of the evergreen leaves of *Berberis* × *gladwynensis* 'William Penn' turned scarlet in winter, I decided to echo this with a coral-bark maple (*Acer palmatum* 'Sangokaku') coppiced annually to encourage maximum production of bright red new stems, a treatment I recommend only where the growing season is long enough and the weather warm and wet enough to encourage six feet or more of growth within a single season.

Encouraged by the cheerful show this pair put on, I planted a sunny corner of my garden for winter cheer. Through the red, scarlet, and yellow canelike stems of dogwoods and willows (*Cornus alba* 'Sibirica', *Salix alba* 'Britzensis', and *Cornus stolonifera* 'Silver and Gold' respectively) I see the yellow-edged leaves of a large shrub, *Elaeagnus* × *ebbingei* 'Gilt Edge', and the copious quantities of scarlet berries on a Burford holly (*Ilex cornuta* 'Burfordii') growing in my neighbor's garden but encouraged to overhang and thrust its branches through the dividing fence. Tall grasses (*Miscanthus sinensis* 'Silberpfeil' and 'Morning Light') add further interest, and in very early spring scarlet tulips (hybrids of *Tulipa kaufmanniana,* long-lived and multiplying) add a further colorful note. Earlier still, in February and March, come orange and yellow crocuses (*Crocus chrysanthus*), tucked in at the front where a late-blooming, blue-flowered dieback shrub (*Ceratostigma willmottianum*) will later emerge to fill the gap.

Coordinated color does not necessitate an unchanging year-long theme. The corner of my garden just described forms part of a semicircular border where, from late May through autumn, the keynote color is pink. The holly ripens its berries in summer and the yellow-variegated elaeagnus is evergreen, so unwanted hot colors are there but they are concealed. The dogwoods and willow give me double mileage: all winter their bare stems have been prominent color notes but by June they have become substantial, densely leafy green bushes, backgrounds for the summer flowers, screening out what lies behind. The unremarkable flowers of the dog-woods are white, followed by white or blue-tinted berries. They get screening help from grasses wearing their summer dress of white and green, and now a new echo comes into play between the white-striped grasses and the white-margined leaves of *Cornus stolonifera* 'Silver and Gold', which do not scorch in hot summer sun as those of the red-stemmed but otherwise similar *Cornus alba* 'Elegantissima' often do in southern gardens. A whole new echo game is, in fact, now getting under way, kicked off by the big white flower knobs that top the five-foot stalks of *Allium multibulbosum* (syn. *A. nigrum*), displayed against the backdrop of *Miscanthus sinensis* 'Morning Light'. In front of the allium is another grass, the creamy white gardener's garters (*Phalaris arundinacea* 'Feesey's Variety'), which spreads a bit less rapidly than the similar *P. a.* 'Variegata'. This disguises the large leaves of the onion which, handsome a month earlier, are now getting shabby as they prepare to die away.

One caveat about *Cornus stolonifera* 'Silver and Gold', lest someone later says "Why didn't you warn me?" The warning is, in fact, intrinsic in the name: any plant called *stolonifera* should be treated with caution, considered guilty until it proves its innocence. *Cornus stolonifera,* a wide-ranging North American species sometimes called red osier, remarking its similarity to some osiers, or willows, is a red-stemmed suckering shrub of rapid spread, especially in moist soil. *Cornus alba,* its Asian cousin, sometimes called Tatarian dog-wood, is not stoloniferous. It is too soon for me to say whether this yellow-stemmed form of red osier will run as rapidly: it will have to spread like wildfire before I'd consider parting with it.

A recent addition to shrubs grown for their winter bark is just becoming available in America. *Cornus alba* 'Winter Flame' is heralded as being the best combination yet of brilliant autumn color and scarlet winter bark. This would be a particularly good choice in a setting devoted to hot colors, as well as for those regions where no flowers remain at this

time of year. Pink flowers continue through November in the winter corner of my garden, so I'm glad that the dogwoods and willow mentioned aren't among those now garbed in scarlet and yellow. I wouldn't, however, discard them if they were. Autumn's pyrotechnic display is too brief to be taken seriously for echo purposes. Better to just enjoy it and not fret if it puts color schemes briefly out of whack, as it does as often as not where there are flowers still around. Berries, too, can be less than harmonious.

If you do find this brief disruption of a color composition bothersome, choose your trees and shrubs accordingly: use those that don't have red berries or red and yellow leaves where what you had in mind was a cooler composition. Choose a magnolia, a styrax, a fringe tree (*Chionanthus*), or

The large flower heads of *Allium nigrum* (syn. *A. multibulbosum*) are set against the very fine, white-striped blades of *Miscanthus* 'Morning Light'. The broad, gray-green leaves of this ornamental onion emerge very early in the year and also die away early. *Artemisia* 'Powis Castle', cut back hard in late winter, grows in front and soon spreads out to cover the empty space. The seed heads of the onion rise well above it, remaining attractive long after the leaves have gone. (My garden; May)

a Chinese elm (*Ulmus parviflora*), for instance, instead of a maple, crepe myrtle, or dogwood, and use shrubs such as the callicarpas with white or violet fruits.

The not-very-cold-hardy *Salvia leucantha,* a rather tender shrubby perennial with white flowers extruded from velvety violet calyces, has endured the worst that winter brings for some fifteen years in one part of my garden but efforts to establish it elsewhere have consistently failed. I go on trying, buoyed by the desire to bring it together with the purple-violet berries of *Callicarpa dichotoma,* the duo then to be underplanted with a little late-blooming purple-flowered onion, *Allium thunbergii* 'Ozawa'. Thinking about this recently, I realized that an equally happy marriage could be made with a white-fruited callicarpa and an underplanting of the white-

In autumn the carpeting juniper surrounding a crepe myrtle (*Lagerstroemia fauriei*) is almost hidden by the red, orange, and yellow fallen leaves. These colors are repeated in the orange berries of *Pyracantha* 'Mohave' and the yellow stripes in the yucca leaves (*Yucca* 'Bright Edge').

flowered form of *Allium thunbergii.* If Mohammed won't come to the mountain, perhaps the mountain can be brought to Mohammed, with which in mind a mountainous clump of miscanthus has just been removed from behind the thriving salvia to make space for a callicarpa. The most successful hot-color autumnal berry-foliage echo in my garden—part accident, part design, comes when the leaves of a crepe myrtle (*Lagerstroemia fauriei*) tumble in an array of scarlet, yellow, crimson, and brown over a carpet of blue-green juniper interplanted with orange-berried *Pyracantha* 'Mohave' (clipped annually to maintain it as a two-foot-high bush of loosely mounded shape) and pierced by clumps of yellow-striped *Yucca* 'Golden Sword'.

The most useful books I know for checking fall color, berry color, and other characteristics of shrubs and trees are *The Hillier Manual of Trees & Shrubs* and Michael Dirr's *Manual of Woody Landscape Plants,* both essential books in any home reference library.

Echoes with Structure and Ornament

Do think about the color of buildings when deciding where to place shrubs with colorful fruits or autumn foliage. The most brilliant of all autumn color comes from the winged euonymus (*Euonymus alatus*). I like best to see this surrounded by plenty of green, or against gray stone walls, but I've seen it looking quite good against a brick wall of dark purplish red. A pyracantha or holly would be a good match for orange-colored brick.

A lot of echo opportunities lie fallow in structural features and garden ornaments. Sometimes they are wasted opportunities, sometimes worse, as witness the countless strings of screaming magenta azaleas lined against red brick walls in the Southeast. No use criticizing if one can't offer a solution, but in this case that's easy to do. If one can't do better, white

A band of lily-flowered tulips, 'White Triumphator', echoes the white sidings of the house in a composition that is simple, fresh, and springlike. (Colonial Williamsburg, Virginia; May)

would draw attention to itself and away from the brick, but this particular eyesore is seen in the very region where gardeners are spoiled for choice among evergreen azaleas. The exact color of red brick varies a good deal, so echo possibilities need to be assessed on the spot. Bicolor flowers are the most likely candidates, and 'Ben Morrison' would often be a good selection. Its book description is "pale scarlet red with white feathered edge and prominent red blotch." Its eye effect, however, leans toward terra-cotta, as does much red brick.

Nowadays there's an almost infinite range of tints available in interlocking concrete paving blocks, including a gray just faintly tinted with purple. Purple foliage is quite difficult to display well at ground level and I've tended to consider gray almost requisite for setting off such low-growing plants

A favorite color can be one's "signature tune." In this case the color was cranberry, used in the interior decor and in paint for the entrance decking, which is echoed by crimson geraniums (*Pelargonium peltatum*) in containers. (Nancy Hook, New York State; July)

as purple ajuga. Seeing *Heuchera* 'Palace Purple' lining a path of the color described opened my mind to other possibilities.

Once in place, paving is usually permanent, and few want to increase the need for maintenance by painting brick house walls. The color of paint trim is more readily changed and even such mundane objects as a garage door can be grist for the colorist's mill: in England I saw one painted yellow, with narrow panels of yellow-centered gold-heart ivy (*Hedera helix* 'Gold Heart") trained on either side. Too gaudy? Then how about a white-variegated ivy (*H.h.* 'Glacier' is a good one) or euonymus (*Euonymus fortunei* 'Gracilis' or *E.f.* 'Silver Queen') to match white shutters and trim?

In Ellen McFarland's Massachusetts garden a white-tipped hemlock, *Tsuga canadensis* 'Gentsch White', echoed a

Above
Pastel salmon bearded iris 'Marriage
Vows' echoes and accentuates the
slight tint added to give warmth to the
concrete paving slabs. Red coralbells
(*Heuchera*) add contrast in color and
form. (Harland Hand for Mr. and
Mrs. D. Lennette, Bay Area,
California; May)

Right
Sequential echoes. The barn red roof
of the birdhouse unites it with the
coppery red young leaves and purple-
tinted flower buds of *Photinia × fraseri*.
When the buds open to white flowers
they'll find a waiting echo partner in
the white parts of the birdhouse.
(Gladys Huyghe, Virginia; May)

Left
Ornamental grasses have so recently sprung upon the horticultural scene that we are still learning how to use them effectively, especially on a small scale. Here is a fine example, with the buff flower spikes of *Calamagrostis acutiflora* 'Karl Foerster' well defined as a pale echo of the brown house sidings and paintwork. (Elise Laurenzi, Massachusetts; August)

Below
Tawny daylilies (*Hemerocallis fulva*) partner the tawny paint of the pagoda. (Ladew Topiary Gardens, Maryland; July)

Above
An imaginative combination of plants and ornament, with tulips on the urn echoed by the real thing and color echoes from the greens and whites in the urn, tulips, and pansies. (Ryan Gainey, Georgia; April)

Right
Hen-and-chickens (*Sempervivum*) are usually grown for their foliage rosettes, not for their flowers, but here, by design or by chance, shared colors of purple and buff in the rocks, the flowers, and the foliage make for echoes of subtle appeal. (Louise Kappus, Ontario, Canada; July)

white gate and picket fence. The graceful birches are among the most popular of ornamental trees and *Betula pendula* 'Purpurea', a slow-growing, purple-leaved form of the European silver birch, was a particularly good choice against the light gray-brown stone and chocolate brown paintwork of an English house.

"I could do that" is often my thought when visiting other gardens. Not, usually, with exact repetition in mind, but rather the sudden recognition of a way of solving a prob-

These sculpted fish by Katy McFadden Benechi are attached to metal stakes, so they are easy to move around or adjust in number. Here they swim in a pool of love-in-a-mist (*Nigella damascena*), echoing its blue and the deeper blue of anchusa. The pink flowers are dianthus. The gray foliage is *Artemisia* 'Valerie Finnis'. The fish are also available in other colors. (Garden of designer Barbara Ashmun, Portland, Oregon; June/July)

lem that had eluded me, or of exploiting an opportunity previously unrecognized.

Serendipitous Echoes

Opposite page
A self-sown foxglove has squeezed itself into a nonexistent space to create an echo with the hardy orchid (*Bletilla striata*) in an east-facing bed with sun for only two hours in the morning. (My garden; May)

Below
Serendipity! It takes more than gardening skills to persuade a cat to pose so prettily among the white daisies (*Chrysanthemum leucanthemum* 'May Queen'). (Gladys Huyghe, Virginia; May)

Honest gardeners will often admit that the only part they played in a combination being admired was to let things be when, for instance, a purple foxglove sowed itself among a patch of the deeper purple hardy orchid (*Bletilla striata*) in my garden, matched further along the border by another self-sown annual or biennial, one of the catchflies, *Silene virginica*, a cottage garden plant with the folk name none-so-pretty. I wouldn't go that far with my praise but I do appreciate the way it tucks itself into small spaces without appearing crowded or smothering other plants, enlivening odd corners

with its small domes of vivid pink flowers—"pretty" is too vapid a word—on branching, wiry stems, of flypaper stickiness just below the flower domes, clad in small glaucous leaves. Once in the garden it self-sows, making do with poor, shallow soil spurned by more aristocratic plants.

First prize for abundance of self-created echoes goes to the endearing, exasperating, insouciant johnny-jump-ups (*Viola tricolor*) in its sundry forms. From this came two appealing spring and early summer combinations in my garden. *Viola tricolor* 'Helen Mount', a johnny of fairly typical coloring—dark violet, pale violet, and yellow—sowed into the outskirts of a small yellow wallflower (*Erysimum helveticum*). Another, called 'Bowles' Black', has two black upper petals

Opposite page
The yellow eyes in the flowers of *Oenothera speciosa* echo the yellow veining in the leaves of *Canna* 'Striata' ('Pretoria'). (University of North Carolina Arboretum, Raleigh; May)

Below
Viola tricolor 'Helen Mount', self-sown into a yellow wallflower (*Erysimum helveticum*). (My garden; May)

and a yellow eye from which purple "lashes" radiate out over three bright violet lower petals rimmed with black. Having disappeared from the spot I'd prepared for it with loving care, it turned up again mingled with the violet flower spikes of *Salvia* 'May Night', looking, I must say, rather smug at having pulled off the perfect color echo.

One of the nice things about a long-established garden is the increasing frequency of such serendipitous delights. At Montrose, in Hillsborough, North Carolina, I expressed admiration at the skill with which a euphorbia with dark red stems had been mixed with a dark red polyanthus. Nobody would claim credit, as this too was a self-placed seedling. Credit was also disclaimed for *Oenothera speciosa,* whose blush pink flowers have a greeny yellow eye, combined with the chartreuse-veined leaves of *Canna* 'Striata' ('Pretoria') in the border at North Carolina State University. "The oenothera hitchhiked in on the roots of something else," wrote Edith Eddleman. Lovely though the combination was, I daresay it was unwelcome, the oenothera being difficult to keep under control.

Self-Echoes

Some plants provide their own echoes, without benefit of companion. Often a flower incorporates two colors, one a paler tint of the other. The showy trailing verbena called 'Texas Form' is one such plant. The twenty or so individual flowers forming the dome-shaped clusters each have two crimson upper petals, echoed by the paler pink of the three lower ones. The upper part of each flower faces inward, resulting in a ring of crimson surrounded by pale pink. Managing to be both delicate and showy, it brightens areas of green where spring flowers have flung their fling, and looks even lovelier against the gray filigree foliage of *Artemisia* 'Powis Castle', or wandering among clumps of white-striped yucca (*Yucca filamentosa* 'Variegata'). If you feel disposed to make an echo marriage, *Rosa* 'Betty Prior' has staying power similar to that of the verbena. Both have a big burst of bloom in early summer, continuing spasmodically until frost brings the season to an end.

In the United States the carpeting phlox (*Phlox subulata*) introduced from Tasmania under the tongue-twisting name of 'Tamanonagalei' was quickly rechristened 'Candy Stripe', a more memorable and much more commercial name. With or without the change, it was destined for instant popularity. The flowers are usually blush pink with darker pink stripes, but not infrequently it sports flowers of solid color that echo the stripes. This can't be counted on but the combination could be deliberately contrived by interplanting 'Tamanonagalei' with one of the several available solid pink selections.

Phlox subulata 'Tamanonagalei' ('Candy Stripe') sporting to solid color. (My garden; April)

The chocolate markings on *Lilium* 'Brushstroke' are presented to perfection against the brownish foliage of *Weigela florida* 'Foliis Purpureis', also called 'Java Red', a comparatively dwarf weigela with flowers of a dusky pink. Having found this lily in a catalogue, I couldn't resist another one called 'Flirt'. This has the same starry form and dark brushmarks but on a background of palest primrose yellow. (Eleanor Carnwath, Seattle, Washington; June)

Echoes also come about effortlessly in many mixed strains of annuals. Sweet alyssum (*Iberis umbellata*) and globe amaranth (*Gomphrena globosa*) both come in mixtures that blend lavenders, lilacs, and purples, a good starting point for additional plants in any of these colors. There are also two separate named strains of globe amaranth that make excellent echo partners: 'Buddy Purple' and the paler 'Lavender Lady'. Globe amaranth is an old-fashioned annual that thrives in summer heat and has long been popular in southern gardens, where it goes on flowering through autumn and then combines well with the purple color forms of ornamental cabbage sold for late-season bedding. The bicolored poor-man's orchids (*Schizanthus*) come in harmonized mixes of crimson and

blued pink, and a packet of mixed calliopsis seed (*Coreopsis tinctoria*) will probably yield some yellow flowers with mahogany centers and others of solid mahogany red. If the seed packet picture is to be believed, you'll get complex banded echo combinations from *Chrysanthemum carinatum:* red with yellow bands, yellow with red bands, and apricot with bands of both red and yellow. The one time I grew them, however, I got only two kinds. Grow purple and white foxgloves together and after a year or two of bee-crosses you'll probably get a blended range of purples, purplish pinks, and pale pinks.

A variegated form of biennial honesty, *Lunaria annua* 'Variegata', combines white flowers with a white-edged leaf. There's more than one variegated form of money plant, some of them a scrambled mix of colors and some with purple flowers, so read descriptions carefully or beg seed or seedlings (there's sure to be plenty to spare) from any garden where you spot the form you want. If you grow this from seed, don't throw out the plain-leaved seedlings in disgust: the name *annua* notwithstanding, it is a biennial, and the variegation often doesn't show until the second year. If kept well away from other forms, seedlings remain in character.

Flowers with
Exceptional Echo Potential

Lilies, daylilies, pansies, and tulips are particularly versatile flowers for creating color echoes. They come in such a wide range of colors that chances are good you'll find just what you want. The blooms of many of them include more than one color. About the only color lacking in daylilies, lilies, and tulips is blue. Bearded irises might fill that color gap where days stay cool during their flowering time. In hot regions bloom time is usually over in a flash, something I deeply regret because their echo potential is otherwise second only to that of daylilies.

Try a dark Bordeaux red lily such as 'Othello' against

The perfect daylily companion for *Achillea* 'Salmon Beauty' is being sought. Because they contrast so markedly in form, yarrows pair well with daylilies. (Virginia; July)

the feathery plumes of a pale pink astilbe, or a yellow one matched to the yellow in the leaves of such variegated shrubs as many selections of holly and euonymus. Put a dusky-eyed daylily against such purple-leaved shrubs as *Cotinus coggygria* 'Royal Purple', a purple barberry, or the grayed purple of *Rosa glauca*.

Because daylilies recognize no rules about what colors go with what, they can point the way to unexpected combinations that carry a garden beyond the mundane. Joanne Walkovic's Pennsylvania garden is small and she squeezes into it many different plants, but she can always be counted on for some well-considered and artistic combinations. One that caught my eye was the deep red *Monarda* 'Adam' paired with

Hemerocallis 'Aabachee', a spidery daylily of matching red with alternate petals edged with white. One of my daylilies has a crimson-purple eye band on a background of that pastel orangy pink variously described as peach, persimmon, or melon, which, on the color chart, is a pale version of carrot. I wish I could tell you its name but it came mislabeled, an altogether too common happening, alas, and another good reason for growing new plants in a nursery bed until you are sure that they are what they are supposed to be. This one looks surprisingly good with the dark wine purple of the drumstick onion, *Allium sphaerocephalon,* or the pincushion-like crimson-purple flowers of *Knautia macedonica.* If you'd prefer a more conventional combination, then the light grape purple of the daylily called 'Little Grapette' combines nicely with the aforementioned ornamental onion. Because their flower shapes contrast markedly, achilleas and daylilies combine extremely well: browse through a daylily catalogue and a hundred likely combinations will suggest themselves.

Green is always present in a garden, so flowers with

Hemerocallis 'Bonanza' has been around for a long time but can still compete with all the gorgeous newcomers as a good garden plant. In this picture its dark eye is matched to annual purple perilla (*Perilla frutescens* 'Crispa'). (My garden; July)

Right
Hemerocallis 'Amersham' (suspiciously similar to 'Stafford', 'Nashville', and 'Eric the Red') is a perfect match for *Helenium* 'Moerheim Beauty'. Their cheerful color is set off to full advantage by *Alchemilla mollis, Eryngium giganteum,* and a few arching sprays of an elegant grass, *Stipa gigantea.* (Mrs. J. R. McCutchan, Bates Green Farm, Sussex, England; August)

Below
As if seeking closer color accord, *Hemerocallis* 'Corky', a daylily of unsurpassed refinement, displays the mahogany coloration on the outside of its petals as it leans over a purple barberry. (Eleanor Carnwath, Seattle, Washington; June)

Above
Tulips come in just about every color
except blue, making it easy to
compose echoes. Here they are
matched to *Thalictrum aquilegifolium,*
itself available in several colors, from
white through pink to varying shades
of lilac and purple. (Longwood
Gardens, Pennsylvania; June)

Left
When tulip 'Georgette' first opens it is
solid yellow, gradually developing
tints of red and orange. Behind the
tulips *Spiraea* 'Golden Princess' forms
mounds of yellow foliage, tipped in
spring with coppery pink. (My garden;
May)

A group of twenty-five 'Angel' tulips is sandwiched between a glossy-leaved, white-flowered shrub, *Choisya ternata,* or Mexican orange, and *Trachelospermum asiaticum* 'Variegatum', one of the daintiest variegated plants but not very hardy, vining if left to its own devices, mounding if given a haircut once in a while. (My garden; April)

green in their makeup can't help but create echoes. Viridiflora tulips are well nigh perfect echo plants, with brevity of bloom their only shortcoming. "Viridiflora" means green-flowered but in actuality the green takes the form of stripes or feathering on another base color: 'Golden Artist' is yellow with green stripes, 'Greenland' is old rose, striped green. My favorites are 'Spring Green' and the similar 'Angel', which are white feathered with a green as fresh and lovely as spring itself, needing only a green background for a cool, refreshing echo. At Stonecrop Caroline Burgess combined 'Spring Green' with variegated Solomon's seal (*Polygonatum odoratum* 'Variegatum'), which bears its little greeny white bells at the same time.

Foliage Echoes

Most flowers, alas, are fleeting—perhaps that makes them the more appreciated. The longest-lasting echoes come from foliage. Many examples are illustrated with the subsequent discussion of basic blender colors. With evergreens such echoes can last the year around as the photo of *Taxus bacatta* 'Standishii' below demonstrates.

    The very best echo plants are those with variegated fo-

There is excellent contrast in form in this stunning combination. Reflected in a small pool, the color glows in the early evening light. *Taxus baccata* 'Standishii' is evergreen. *Carex elata* 'Bowles' Golden' usually isn't, but a year-round echo could be achieved by replacing it with the evergreen golden variegated sweet flag, *Acorus gramineus* 'Ogon', a plant that is at its most luxurious in moist soil but tolerates average to dry conditions. (Rex Murfitt, Victoria, Canada; June)

liage. Strolling around my garden early one May morning, cup of tea in hand, I stopped, spellbound, when I passed under *Styrax japonica*. Flowers had showered down during the night and now, starlike, intact and unsullied, lay scattered over hummocks of a favorite sedge, *Carex conica* 'Marginata', which has slender, arching blades finely edged with white.

This was an unexpected and unplanned echo, but white flowers against white-edged leaves is a combination that seldom fails to delight. "Never," I once would have said, but in gardening, as in life in general, "Never say never, and never say always" is sage advice. A newly acquired cultivar of *Liriope japonica* with white flowers and variegated leaves has been a bit disappointing, though I may yet learn how to use it well. There is inadequate contrast, and it gets a low mark when compared with either the variegated form with purple flowers, or the white flowers and dark green foliage of *L.* 'Monroe's White'. Another cause for dissatisfaction is that the leaf variegation is creamy rather than white. I'm

Echoes employing two foliage plants are effective for a much longer time than those utilizing flowers. Caroline Burgess interplanted *Lamium* 'White Nancy' with *Brunnera macrophylla* 'Langtrees', also known as 'Aluminium Spot' (English name, English spelling), for an echo of shape and color, with contrast in size. Most who don't like spotted and speckled variegations make an exception for the even patterning of this brunnera. (Stonecrop, New York; July)

inclined to say that when white flowers are combined with variegated leaves, it must be a clean white variegation. But saying "always" all but guarantees that I'll encounter exceptions soon thereafter.

"The woods are lovely—dark and deep," wrote Robert Frost. This makes a woodland garden a refreshing retreat from hot summer weather. Dark, however, is not what flowers want, so once the trees leaf out interest and contrast must come mainly from foliage. In such settings white variegations really shine out, and most such plants like or tolerate shade. Early in the year white flowers could create echoes: imagine snowdrops through a carpet of such small ivies as 'Little Diamond'. When the flowers have gone to rest, white from the leaves remains. White-edged hostas spaced among sweet woodruff (a rapid spreader, not for use in limited space or among small, fragile plants) makes a combination as refreshing as lemonade, and more appealing, if less fascinating to collectors, than lots of different hostas growing cheek by jowl.

Green-leaved plants in this picture include ferns, hostas, *Petasites japonicus*, rhododendrons, and other shrubs. Plants with white variegations include hostas, variegated pachysandra, the ivy 'Glacier', and *Lamiastrum* 'Herman's Pride'. (Susan Dumaine, Massachusetts; September)

In this captivating, bridelike combination, the dainty flowers on arching branches of the shrubby *Deutzia gracilis* flow over the bold, white-edged leaves of *Hosta undulata* 'Albomarginata'. Further back the white is repeated with sweet woodruff (*Galium odoratum*), with just a touch of color contrast from blue *Phlox divaricata* (Joanne Reed, Pennsylvania; May)

Be aware that the white variegation in many leaves is creamy when the leaves first emerge in spring. I have an herbaceous sedge, *Carex siderosticta* 'Variegata', growing in front of *Euonymus fortunei* 'Emerald Gaiety', both of which start off creamy, then become whiter. In this case the combination works well because they make the change more or less in unison. A hosta on my present (ever-changing) list of "best ten," 'So Sweet' (and sweet it is, in appearance and slightly so in fragrance), starts its season with creamy variegation but by the time the white flowers appear much later on, this has long since turned to white. At its creamy stage an echo could be contrived with an early-flowering cream astilbe.

I'm shooting for a triple with *Euonymus* 'Emerald Gaiety'. In February and March the variegation is still white, and behind it the early white flowers of a quince, *Chaenomeles*

'Jet Trail', are now opening. A white starflower, *Ipheion uniflorum* 'Graystone White', also flowers at this time and will be moved to join them. For Act II, when the euonymus briefly wears its creamy new garb, I'm seeking an early-blooming perennial, not too big, with creamy flowers (suggestions welcomed). Act III, when the euonymus is white again, will be easy: a late-blooming white chrysanthemum.

Occasionally a white-variegated plant does things the other way around, starting off white, becoming cream. *Arundo donax* 'Variegata' is one of these. Early in the season it can echo such white phloxes as 'Miss Lingard', 'Mt. Fuji', and the recently introduced 'David' which is said to be mildew-free. In July, with its variegation turned to rich cream, it echoed the pastel yellow flowers of *Abelmoschus* (usually listed as *Hibiscus*) 'Manihot Lemon Bowl' in the border at North Carolina State University.

Different plants, different season, but a similar effect to that in the last picture. The white flowers of *Lespedeza thunbergii* 'White Fountain' cascade over *Yucca filamentosa* 'Variegata', which in turn is underplanted with *Zephyranthes candida,* one of the best summer and autumn flowering bulbs for southern gardens. (My garden; September)

When used in "white" gardens, variegated plants help break up too big an expanse of unrelieved white, while still fitting perfectly into the scheme of things. White gardens often include touches of such pastel colors as lavender and creamy or pale lemon yellows. Here the variegated *Phlox* 'North Leigh', which later bears pale lilac flowers, is combined with lilies, hostas, *Campanula latifolia* 'Alba', *Astrantia major,* and *Centranthus ruber* 'Alba'. (Barbara Flynn, Seattle, Washington; Late June)

There's an enormous range of hostas with leaves bicolored in innumerable different patternings of green, blue-green, chartreuse, white, cream, and gold. For its crisp, white variegation and its easygoing ways, I continue to favor the old *Hosta undulata* 'Albomarginata', but a growing number of other kinds vie with it for my affection.

The latest of these is *Hosta fluctuans* 'Variegata'. Don't follow the usual (and usually good) dictum that perennials should go in groups of three or more: this hosta should form a group of one, it would be a shame to cram it in among other plants. My two-year-old clump, starting from gallon-can size, measures three feet across and about fifteen inches high. The undulating leaves, spaced well apart on sturdy gray petioles, have edges brushed with ivory. In front of it grow fans of a slender-bladed, cream-edged Japanese sweet flag (*Acorus gramineus* 'Variegatus') and, early in the year, yellow primroses. Behind, not too close, stands a hefty, upright clump, six feet high, of an ivory-flowered form of *Iris pseudacorus*. Mine was grown from seed but forms of similar color can be bought as *I.p.* 'Bastardii' or 'Turnip Seed'. Over a period of at least four weeks—a very long time for an iris— it bore hundreds of flowers. So much admiration did this combination attract that it was instrumental in the introduction of my garden's very first seat, a simple red cedar log bench, on which to sit and enjoy it. The leaves of the iris remain attractive all season, which is more than can be said for bearded irises. Yellow flags are such prolific self-sowers and naturalizers that I wouldn't be surprised to see them follow purple loosestrife onto the list of plants we are not permitted to grow because they crowd out native kinds. Remove the seed pods, which takes only a few minutes, and there is no problem.

A good way of displaying hostas is to have them rise out of a carpeting plant of matching or contrasting color. One with white in its leaves could be underplanted with *Mazus reptans* 'Alba' or white-flowered periwinkle (*Vinca minor* 'Alba' or, in small spaces, the more compact *V.m.* 'Ger-

trude Jekyll'). One with creamy or chartreuse-yellow variegation could grow through Scotch moss (*Sagina subulata*
'Aurea') or yellow creeping charlie (*Lysimachia nummularia*
'Aurea'). All these plants prefer moist, humus-rich soil and
a lightly shaded situation. It can also work well to reverse
this and interplant something else to grow through a group
of hostas. One such combination in my garden looks cool
and fresh from spring well into autumn—no mean accom-
plishment when much else, including me, is wilting in the
heat. The duet consists of white-edged *Hosta* 'Francee' interplanted with *Oxalis rubra* 'Alba', a gem of a plant for light
shade, dainty enough not to crowd the hostas, yet tough and
showy enough to command its share of light and homage.

The picture shows one clump from a
group of three *Hosta* 'Francee'
interplanted with *Oxalis rubra* 'Alba'.
(My garden; June.)

73

For sunny sites and dry soil, junipers are hard to beat. *Juniperus davurica* 'Expansa Variegata' and the similar but slower-growing *J.d.* 'Expansa Aureospicata' have flattened sprays of foliage flecked with cream and yellow respectively. In these the variegation is constant, never becoming white. Both make wide-spreading shrubs, horizontal at first, becoming mounded in time. The Warminster broom (*Cytisus × praecox* 'Warminster'), with showers of creamy yellow flowers in spring or early summer, thrives in similar conditions and would make a good companion for either of these junipers.

One pretty, hardy, and adaptable shrub with cream-variegated leaves is, I see, among the long list of those that have suffered a recent name change. What I know as *Acanthopanax sieboldianus* 'Variegatus' is now, it seems, *Eleutherococcus*. May heaven help gardeners struggling to keep up with taxonomists. I find myself increasingly in sympathy with those who insist on common names. Unfortunately,

The base color of *Hosta* 'Shade Fanfare' matches that of creeping charlie (*Lysimachia nummularia* 'Aurea') but the white edges to the hosta leaves make it visually distinct from the underplanting. A good companion for these, set behind the hosta, would be *Aquilegia canadensis,* or some similar columbine combining scarlet and yellow or cream in its flowers. (Garden of the late Richard Meyer, Ohio; July)

there often isn't one. Donald Wyman, in *Shrubs and Vines for American Gardens,* calls the species (which has all green leaves) five-leaved aralia, but it isn't an aralia (not at present, anyway!), though it is in the same family. In any event, it is beautiful. I've found it trouble-free through hot and humid summers and Donald Wyman reports the species to be hardy in zone 4, further reporting that the leaves remain on the plant long into the fall and that it has the admirable trait of growing well in shade and withstanding city growing conditions. It is a medium-sized shrub that could, in the long term, be trained into a small tree. It can also be kept pruned to small-shrub size if you prefer. The palmate leaves are broadly margined in rich cream, the centers marbled in two shades of green. There are small curved prickles at the leaf bases but I wouldn't call it a scratchy shrub. During its sojourn in my garden it has done well on a slightly raised knoll in dryish shade beneath the spreading branches of a large oak.

The large, clean-cut white daisies of the early Shasta daisy 'May Queen' are well set off against the white-striped blades of *Miscanthus sinensis* 'Variegatus'. If kept deadheaded, the daisy flowers for a very long time. (My garden; May)

Ajuga 'Burgundy Glow' has moved itself out of the bed in which it was planted into the moister soil of the mulch path. The flowers providing the pink echo are *Oxalis brasiliensis,* which blooms in late spring or early summer and then goes dormant, reappearing in late autumn. (My garden; June)

It would, I suspect, scorch in full hot summer sun. Its companion needs more moisture, a requirement satisfied in part by providing rich soil at the base of the knoll and lining the planting holes with layers of newspaper. Here grows a sedge (*Carex*) called 'Frosted Curls', its dense, arching clumps of hair-fine blades a mound of shimmering green, platinum, and cream.

Perennials with pink variegations in the leaves are rather few, and these are seldom tough or carefree plants. The best I know is *Ajuga reptans* 'Burgundy Glow'. It needs soil that doesn't get dry, and shade in hot regions. Rosettes reverting to green or purple need to be removed fairly frequently, and it isn't as cold hardy as most other ajugas, but plants of such exceptional qualities amply reward a little extra care. At Stonecrop one border terminated in an apron of this ajuga, overhung by the trailing red chenille tassels of that old-fashioned annual called love-lies-bleeding (*Amaranthus caudatus*). I bought another ajuga recently, called 'Pink Silver', described as being more vigorous than 'Burgundy Glow'. It does seem to be a tougher plant, less demanding of moisture and less inclined to revert to green. Through it grows a wee tulip, *Tulipa pulchella* 'Persian Pearl', with crocuslike, yellow-eyed purple flowers very early in spring. This precocious little poppet is only six inches high and growing it through a ground cover saves the flowers from mud splash.

Lack of hardiness is not the problem with *Houttuynia cordata* 'Chameleon'. It is not many years since this plant made its debut at garden centers, where the showy creamy yellow and bright pink variegation made it an instant success. It is, alas, extremely invasive, and many have come to rue the day they planted it. If you succumb, treat it as you would a running bamboo, making sure that its roots are totally confined. In one practical and pleasing partnership it was used as ground cover on a small island in a pond, interplanted with clumps of *Iris pseudacorus* 'Variegatus', which has yellow-striped leaves in spring.

The pink-variegated culinary sage, *Salvia officinalis* 'Tri-

76

color', is a very beautiful and popular plant, but seldom a long-lived one. In cold regions it is killed back in winter and may or may not regrow in spring. Zone numbers aren't helpful in assessing its hardiness because there are factors in play other than temperature, such as lack of winter snow, soggy soil, or bitter winds. It dislikes humid summers and is apt to drown in the combination of torrential rain and high temperature that brings that condition about. It helps to place flat rocks or paving stones over its roots to protect against extremes of wet or cold.

There's a bigger range of shrubs and trees with some pink in their leaves, including a good many Japanese maples. There are many beautiful pastel color forms of the English

The owners of this garden hold a British collection of old pinks and carnations, many of which could echo the pink coloring of *Salvia officinalis* 'Tricolor'. In this instance its companion plant is a pink-flowered helianthemum. (Mr. and Mrs. M. Hughes, Herefordshire, England; June)

primrose, *Primula vulgaris,* and these make pretty underplant-ings for maples such as the popular and readily available *Acer palmatum* 'Butterfly', which at primrose time has pink tints in its dainty white-variegated leaves. The color may vary from one region to another. In my garden the pink leans toward terra-cotta, emphasized by an underplanting of Barn-haven primroses of similar color.

Japanese maples have surprised me with their tolerance of heat, and even of hot sun. Many other variegated shrubs have proved less adaptable, and pink variegations seem more inclined to scorch than yellow or white ones. There are, how-ever, some tiptop pink-variegated shrubs for echo purposes where the weather permits them to give of their best. *Cornus florida* 'Welchii' is a delicious confection of white, pink, and soft green, and *Acer negundo* 'Flamingo' equally covetable. *Ajuga* 'Burgundy Glow' would be a good underplanting for either of these.

Hypericum × *moserianum* 'Tricolor' is a charming small shrub or subshrub (it usually dies to the ground in winter), with little leaves of cream and green edged with pink that are colorful from the moment new shoots emerge at ground level very early in spring. It comes cheerfully through hot summers but is a bit on the tender side, probably only long-term hardy where the temperature seldom drops to zero degrees Fahr-enheit. It roots easily from cuttings and grows quite fast, so it is worth overwintering in a greenhouse, frame, under lights, or on a sunny windowsill.

Berberis thunbergii 'Rose Glow' isn't the least bit tem-peramental. It takes heat and cold in its stride and isn't fussy about soil or site. Hillier's *Manual of Trees and Shrubs* says it was selected in Holland about 1957 but is "now superseded by other forms." I'm inclined to take their word as gospel, and to covet 'Harlequin' (with leaves smaller than those of 'Rose Glow' and more heavily mottled pink) and 'Pink Queen' (the best pink variegated form), but these haven't yet come into my orbit, nor are they listed in the Andersen Hor-ticultural Library's Source List (purchasable from Minnesota

Landscape Arboretum, 3675 Arboretum Drive, Chanhassen, MN 55317), and 'Rose Glow' will take a lot of beating. The pink marbling in its purple leaves makes it a prime candidate for echoes. In the Seattle garden of Glenn Withey and Charles Price it formed the background for dark wine red lilies (possibly 'Othello'). In the Vermont garden of Wayne Winterrowd and Joe Eck it was equally bewitching faced down with pink-and-blue *Salvia viridis* (formerly called *Salvia horminum*), the pink echoing the patterning in the barberry leaves, the blue providing contrast without competition. If, in seeking to emulate this, you order seed from a catalogue that uses popular names, read the descriptions carefully. In the United States the name "clary" has been filched from the much taller *Salvia sclarea,* where it properly belongs, and applied to *S. viridis*.

There aren't many vines with pink in their foliage. The showiest I know is a tricolored kiwi vine, *Actinidia kolomikta*. Kiwi flowers tend to hide under the leaves and could easily be missed but I've never noticed flowers on this and *Hillier's Manual* suggests that the form in cultivation is a nonflowering male. Flowers might be an anticlimax, anyway, upstaged by the colorful pink, creamy white, and green leaves. The proportion of pink, or white flushed pink, differs from leaf to leaf; sometimes only the tip is colored, often half the leaf in a clearly demarcated line, and occasionally almost all the leaf. Patience is needed, though, because the variegation is usually missing from young plants and may take several years to develop. Patience had paid off in the New York garden of artist Elisabeth Sheldon, a horticultural writer who practices what she preaches, where the dainty pale pink rose 'Ballerina' made a charming companion for the colorful vine. Kiwis are sturdy twining vines and their supports should also be strong. Unlike, for instance, clematis, which need slender supports around which to curl their petioles, kiwis have no problem encircling a two-by-four, though they'll also climb on a wire. If you don't have a place for a suitable support, perhaps there's a tree stump that would be the better for a disguise. In one

Right
Plants in this border include magenta phlox, yellow achillea, scarlet penstemon, and poppies in mixed colors. The repetitive use of blue larkspur unites the colors and carries the eye along. The larkspur was sprinkled in as seed. (Shirley Andreae, Ontario, Canada; July)

Below
No color is excluded from this garden. All merge harmoniously within the uniting groundwork of chartreuse-flowered *Alchemilla mollis*. (Selby Key, Oregon; June)

woodland garden the kiwi rambled over a large stump in a clearing, faced down with pink and white azaleas.

Toning Down Harsh Color, Uniting Mixed Colors

Assorted bright colors can be toned down and bound together with such noncombative colors as green, gray, cream, and some blues. White doesn't do it in solid blocks but sometimes does when used as confettilike sprinklings throughout a planting. Colors that come on too strong can also be toned down with a pale echo of their own color: pastel pink with magenta, for example, or lavender with purple. One plant with which I have a problem is *Liatris* 'Kobold'. It does well for me and asks little in return, demanding no staking, enduring dry spells, and requiring only infrequent division and this very easy to do. Such qualities are not to be scorned, especially in a plant of the none-too-common spirelike form, but I find the color harsh and my plants went through several divorces before a happy marriage was accomplished with the pale lilac flowers of *Monarda fistulosa*. The liatris brings zest to this partnership, the monarda a quieting touch. *Yucca filamentosa* further calms the combination with its gray-green leaves and firmness of form. Even better with the liatris is *Phlox paniculata* 'Sternhimmel' ('Starry Sky'), which has a purple starburst within a white one at the center of each lavender-blue flower. The phlox, however, needs richer soil and more moisture than the liatris demands if mildew is to be staved off.

Turning Liabilities into Assets

Echoes can turn liabilities into assets. Many a plant that, alone or in the wrong setting, lacks appeal, attracts admiration when grouped with thoughtfully chosen companions. So it

A grouping that keeps this corner of the garden well clothed and cheerful through winter: *Mahonia* 'Arthur Menzies', *Aucuba japonica* 'Fructualbo', a chartreuse-berried form of *Nandina domestica,* and an underplanting of *Liriope muscari* 'Variegata'. (My garden; January)

was with a comparatively rare, slow-growing aucuba given to me many years ago. Vacillation about the color of its fruits is apparent in the name, *Aucuba japonica* 'Fructuluteo' (yellow-fruited), having been changed to 'Fructu-albo' (white-fruited). The fruits are actually a very pale greenish yellow and go unnoticed among leaves sparingly spotted and blotched with similar color. Though much less striking than scarlet-berried aucubas, or those with bolder variegation, it merits a place where its smaller size is an asset. Because I'm somewhat averse to mottled variegations, it got shuttled from one inconspicuous corner to another during its ten-year sojourn in my garden—unappreciated but too good to throw away, awaiting an eager adoptee but passed unnoticed by those usually quick to spot and covet the unusual.

And then, one December day, I noticed how well its creamy patterning matched the yellow flowers of *Mahonia* 'Arthur Menzies', and that a yellow-berried nandina (sometimes described as white but, again, really a pale creamy green) would make this a color-matched trio. The nandina bears its berries in large, conspicuous bunches, showy when sunlit but overpowered when grouped, as mine was, with its scarlet-fruited brethren.

Aucubas and nandinas move fairly easily and the group was put together in one afternoon. As is usually the case with assorted shrubs, a uniform ground cover was needed to bind them together. A large patch of variegated liriope was overdue for thinning out so this, with its grassy cream-striped blades, was the obvious candidate. There were now four different evergreens grouped together, two of them variegated. Theoretically, this results in one of two effects: stodginess if the evergreens are similar in size and form, restlessness if they are not, especially with variegated plants. These four differ markedly in texture and form but the echo effect of the common color unites them into a very satisfying grouping, at its best in midwinter and early spring but attractive all the year, and in harmony with the pink flowers of nearby camellias and the purple ones of azaleas on the other side of the path. A jar of aucuba cuttings on the kitchen counter (aucubas root readily in water) attests to the newfound desirability of the little aucuba so long unloved. This corner of the garden is lightly shaded in summer when nearby oaks are in leaf, so ferns and columbines will be used to fill remaining gaps between the shrubs.

When one changes one's mind about a plant after seeing it in another garden, it does become apparent that there are no bad plants, only failure to use them to good effect. If you share my dislike for spotted or mottled foliage, you might be won over by the dark, pink-polka-dotted leaves of *Hypoestes* 'Pink Splash' underplanted with pale pink impatiens or wax begonias. *Tovara* 'Painter's Palette' has large leaves marbled in green and cream, overprinted with chevrons and blotches of brown and purplish pink. Though not among its fans, I did admire it in combination with the crimson astilbe 'Red Sentinel', and I may yet take it to my garden, if not my heart,

Purple barberries (*Berberis thunbergii*) spaced along the front of this mixed border echo not only each other but also the barn in the background. Early in the year, shrubs hold sway, later there'll be color from perennials. (Ellen and Gordon Penick, Virginia; May)

after seeing it combined with the rosy purple fading bracts of *Euphorbia* × *martinii*.

The beautiful copper-tinted new leaves of easy-to-please *Spiraea japonica* 'Goldflame' make this a shrub seldom missing from the gardens of color schemers. Its Achilles' heel is magenta flowers, incompatible with its yellow foliage and impossible to ignore. Best, then, to acknowledge their presence and provide them with appropriate companions. *Berberis* 'Rose Glow' works quite well; the basic purple of its leaves is compatible with the spiraea's yellowish foliage, the pink marbling with its flowers, and the barberry's own flowers are an inoffensive creamy yellow.

Punctuation, Continuity, Cohesion, and Contrast

Another kind of color echo is punctuation, a time-tested way of bringing continuity, and sometimes a touch of formality, to a border by means of repetition. Punctuation in a border carries the eye along. An uninterrupted edging of a single color does the same thing in a more flowing way. One practical advantage of punctuating a border with such more-or-less permanent plants as shrubs and large grasses is that it breaks the border up into smaller units that are easier to plan and plant than the sometimes intimidating expanse of a big border. It is also easier to rip out and replant a border one section at a time than to redo the whole thing. Punctuation defines the sections without fragmenting the border, making it easier to move from one combination of colors to another without losing continuity.

Many different plants can be used for punctuation, including herbaceous perennials or even annuals, but because they are more constant in color and form and retain some substance in winter, shrubs are often the best choice. If evergreens are used, continuity is maintained when the herbaceous plants are dormant.

84

This is important in regions where gardening doesn't come to a halt in winter and in such regions there is a big range of suitable evergreens. Boxwoods are the choice of many gardeners, but in Southern gardens what is assumed to be boxwood (often by the garden owner as well as the passerby) may be dwarf yaupon (*Ilex vomitoria* 'Nana'), a dwarf cultivar of Japanese holly (*I. crenata*), or the tiny-leaved, compact *Euonymus japonicus* 'Microphyllus'. All of these are amenable to pruning if this is needed to maintain a uniform shape.

In cold regions winter continuity in flower borders is less important, even an undesirable intrusion on an otherwise peaceful snow-blanketed scene. Dead patches are not acceptable in plants being grown for their neat uniformity and the conifers that comprise the hardiest evergreens are slow to regain their good looks if damaged by cold, disease, or light-excluding herbaceous plants. So in the North the choice probably falls on deciduous shrubs or herbaceous plants.

Evergreen *Cupressus sempervirens* 'Swane's Gold' provides the punctuation in this border of softly glowing colors. Other plants include *Agastache* 'Apricot Sunrise', *Hypericum* 'Hidcote', lilies, pansies, snapdragons, and gold-variegated *Salvia officinalis* 'Icterina'. (Virginia and Arnie Israelit, Oregon; June)

Matched shrubs of architectural form, be it block, dome, or column, natural or maintained by pruning, bring a touch of formality to borders when they are placed in line and evenly spaced. Provided plants of appropriate size are used, they can be at the front, the back, or in the middle of a border. Clumping grasses that hold their form when top growth is dead can be used for a softened formality: purple-leaved forms of *Pennisetum setaceum* are particularly effective along the middle of a border. Variegated forms of miscanthus are also excel-

Rhododendrons and azaleas are a major interest of this garden owner. They provide a background for perennials in curved borders surrounding a circular lawn. The effect is a softened formality. Three golden barberries (*Berberis thunbergii* 'Aurea') dotted into this section of the border draw attention to a golden honey locust (*Gleditsia triacanthos* 'Sunburst') in the background. The barberries are young plants and will have to be clipped hard each year to maintain them at this size. Formality is not the intent and punctuation does not continue all around the border. (George McClellan, Virginia; Late April)

lent, as well as being much hardier. Such smaller grasses as *Pennisetum alopecuroides* 'Hameln' could be used along the front.

In an article for *The Green Scene* (the magazine of the Pennsylvania Horticultural Society) published in January 1993, Joanna Reed, who welcomes visitors to her Pennsylvania garden by appointment, writes: "The repetitive use of specific plants, colors, and/or textures throughout a garden makes it cohesive, exciting, and alive." Such repetition can be of a formal, punctuating kind, as just described, or much more casual.

In one of my borders color continuity comes in spring from *Sedum* 'Weihenstephaner Gold', *Erysimum helveticum,* and *Aurinia saxatilis,* all low-growing plants with yellow flowers, visually coherent yet inherently more interesting than repeating the same plant. A yellow columbine (*Aquilegia chrysantha*) and spires of *Thermopsis villosa* repeat the yellow further back. As these fade, there's a second wave of yellows

Twin echoes of bright color from astilbes and *Lythrum* 'Morden's Pink' add excitement to a border in which softer colors predominate. (Elisabeth Sheldon, New York State; July)

87

Above and top of page
These borders certainly don't lack interest. At least ten different kinds of plant can be counted in one small patch. They are welded into a charming tapestry by the repetition of plants and colors, primarily the purple foliage of *Sedum spurium* 'Dragon's Blood' and the many gray-leaved plants. (Louise Kappus, Ontario, Canada; Early August)

along the front from *Oenothera tetragona riparia,* little known but one of the best sundrops, a sundrops look-alike from Texas once classified as an oenothera but now as *Calylophus serrulatus,* and bushy gray-leaved *Hypericum tomentosum,* a plant fairly new to my garden for which I already have a high regard. (I know it is frustrating to read about a plant and not be able to find it—the most likely source for these is Plant Delights Nursery, 9241 Sauls Road, Raleigh, NC 27603.) The second wave of yellow at the back includes achilleas, daylilies, and taller sundrops. The secondary color is blue at first, from irises, veronicas, and tradescantia, overlapped by violet and purple from verbenas and *Salvia × superba* as the season progresses.

Borders in the garden of a friend gain more lasting cohesiveness from clumps of *Sedum × alboroseum* 'Medio-variegatum' evenly spaced along the front. This is one of the showiest plants in the spring garden, its bright creamy yellow variegation visible from afar. It starts the display very early, maintains it late, and needs no maintenance other than occasional division. The budget conscious need buy only one: rooted stems are easily detached, and even small broken-off pieces of stem root with the greatest of ease. The color pales a little as the season progresses, sharing the limelight with later flowers. Each clump can then be developed into an individual composition, employing echoes or contrasts, or both, as you choose. That the flowers are too pallid to attract much attention broadens the usefulness of the plant, for likewise they are too pale to clash with other colors. They can, however, be drawn out of their self-imposed retreat by partnering them with bright pink flowers to give emphasis to the

Two punctuating plants alternate along the front of this border. Creamy-foliaged *Sedum alboroseum* 'Mediovariegatum' would be a good choice in most parts of the country, being cold hardy, heat tolerant, long-lived, easy to grow, and attractive all through the growing season. The bushy mauve-flowered *Erysimum* 'Bowles' Mauve' flowers for a very long time and has attractive gray-green foliage but it is neither very hardy nor very long-lived. (Ellen and Gordon Penick, Virginia; May)

Within a fenced enclosure divorcing hot colors from the main garden, color echoes consist of matched pairs of plants on either side to create symmetry. Plants include achilleas 'Gold Plate' and 'Coronation Gold', *Hemerocallis* 'Stella de Oro', *Lychnis × arkwrightii* 'Vesuvius', *Campanula glomerata, Coreopsis* 'Early Sunrise', gaillardias, heliopsis, *Coreopsis verticillata, Lilium* 'Enchantment', *Heuchera* 'Pluie de Feu', *Cosmos sulphureus, Sanvitalia procumbens,* nasturtiums, and pelargoniums. (Elisabeth Sheldon, New York State; Early July)

pink eyes of the whitish flowers. Fred and Mary Anne McGourty did this very successfully in their Connecticut garden using *Aster* 'Alma Potschke', which flowers at the same time.

The Need for Contrast

My main theme is echoes, and this calls for some kind of similarity, usually but not always in color. Contrast is also important, if not in color then in plant shape or texture or in flower form. If one defines "contrast" in the broadest sense, two tones of the same color can both echo and contrast. One of my favorite plants is *Ranunculus ficaria* 'Brazen Hussy', which bears brassy yellow flowers over ground-hugging rosettes of very dark purplish brown leaves, a color lost against brown earth and needing contrast to set it off. In my garden

90

this contrast takes two very different forms. In one place it grows through yellow-leaved creeping charlie (*Lysimachia nummularia* 'Aurea'), with yellow-chartreuse foliage that makes for effective if somewhat strident contrast. I like it, but prefer the quieter echo-contrast where it grows through the sand-colored gravel of the drive.

Plantings based on harmonious groupings of closely related colors employ less strong color contrast than plantings of mixed colors. The more limited the range of colors, the greater is the need for contrast in form and texture, and this becomes crucial to the success of such monochromatic ventures as white gardens. On a smaller scale, who would have supposed that two kinds of orange marigolds could create an echo? In a shopping plaza in Vail, Colorado, a tall mop-headed hybrid marigold was banked behind the lower growing, dainty, single-flowered *Tagetes tenuifolia,* their flowers the same glowing orange but markedly different in size and

The dark purple-brown foliage of a celandine, *Ranunculus ficaria* 'Brazen Hussy' is pronounced by contrast with the gravel that palely echoes it. (My garden; April)

91

Above
Achillea 'The Beacon' and *Gaillardia* 'Burgundy' echo each other in color while contrasting in form. (My garden; June)

Right
A very satisfying echo of shape and color came from ribbon grass (*Phalaris arundinacea* 'Feesey's Variety') and *Miscanthus* 'Silberpfeil'. There would be insufficient contrast without the space between. (My garden; July)

Above
There is repetition of color but strong textural contrast between *Arundinaria* (*Pleioblastus*) *viridistriata* and *Hosta montana* 'Aureomarginata'. The pretty dwarf bamboo is invasive and needs to be restrained, perhaps by planting it in a sunken container. (Dan Heims, Terra-Nova Nursery, Portland, Oregon; June)

Left
There's a double echo in this clever combination. Gaillardias 'Red Plume' and 'Yellow Plume' provide repetition in shape and contrast in color, while 'Yellow Plume' echoes the color of *Abutilon pictum* 'Thompsonii'. (Denver Botanic Garden, Colorado; September)

White tulips are matched to white-flowered dogwoods. Had all the tulips been white it would have been a pretty scene but it is improved by the matching shape with contrasting color of the pink tulips. (Ellen and Gordon Penick, Virginia; May)

form. A bit gaudy, perhaps, for the home garden, but a spirit-lifting planting in the bright clear light and holiday mood of its setting.

Plants that lack sufficient contrast when adjacent can sometimes echo each other cohesively when there is space, or other plants, between them. I have one such echo where a bright pink form of yarrow (*Achillea millefolium*) grows on one side of a path and *Spiraea japonica* grows on the other side. One is a perennial, the other a shrub, and they differ in foliage and shape, yet the platelike heads of flowers are so similar in color and form that they would merge indistinguishably if placed close together. As it is, though almost a mirror image, each plant retains its separate identity.

94

Space between plants can also disguise slight color differences. I had sought to create an echo with *Aster* 'Purple Dome' at the base of the much taller aster 'Hella Lacy', the contrast coming from their different shapes and heights. It wasn't sufficient, and they differed in color more than I had thought, but when spaced well apart, with white flowers in between, they appear to be identical in color and thereby make that section of border more cohesive.

An echo in my garden that went awry. The flowers of *Daphne* × *burkwoodii* 'Carol Mackie' are faintly tinted with pink and a pink-flowered underplanting (*Ajuga* 'Pink Elf', for instance) would have emphasized this, but in southern heat the daphne's flowers quickly fade to white, so white-flowered *Arabis procurrens* was chosen as underplanting. Although one is a mounding shrub, the other a mat-forming ground cover, the daphne and the arabis proved texturally too similar for the combination—though inoffensive—to do full justice to the plants. (April)

The combination was improved by interplanting the arabis with two white-variegated plants of much stronger form: *Ligularia tussilaginea* 'Argentea' and *Carex* 'Sparkler'. A self-sown Japanese painted fern (*Athyrium niponicum* 'Pictum') added further textural contrast. A variegated hosta could take the place of the ligularia in colder regions.

There are white flowers from a dogwood and sweet woodruff (*Galium odoratum*) but all the other color comes from foliage—from the green of trees, conifers, and hedges, the lighter green of boxwoods and the darker green of germander (*Teucrium chamaedrys*) in the parterre hedging, from the purple of barberries, the chartreuse of a threadleaf cypress (*Chamaecyparis pisifera* 'Filifera Aurea'), and from the variegated leaves of *Weigela florida* 'Variegata'. (Ellen and Gordon Penick, Virginia; May)

The
Colors 3

Unifiers, Blenders, and Foliage Colors

In planning our color schemes we do well to study the landscape and take a leaf from nature's book. Before it is embellished with brighter hues, the basic colors laid on nature's canvas are the green of grass and trees, the brown of the earth (in gardens interpreted with dark, or "purple," foliage), the gray of rocks (and often of skies), the amber of beaches, the white of clouds, and the blue of the sky. These are basic blender colors, the good mixers, seldom seriously out of place. Stark white and bright silver-gray are quite capable of dominating a color conversation but in the main these are the listeners at the party, the pacifiers, the buffers between colliding colors.

Among the blender colors, those found in foliage (green, gray, purple), together with chartreuse, are particularly important. Long-lasting, they form the garden's color infra-

Seldom can so many plants have been packed into such little space with so much artistry, refuting the notion that quantity is incompatible with quality. There are blue flowers, white ones, and pastel tints of other colors from such plants as silvery pink *Geranium* 'Mavis Simpson', but foliage shrubs, grasses, and herbaceous plants are the basis of the border: gray, chartreuse and golden green, and white variegations. There are innumerable echoes and an exhaustive list of plants would fill a page. They include *Hydrangea macrophylla* 'Blue Wave', golden cut-leaved elder (*Sambucus racemosa* 'Plumosa Aurea'), lamb's ears (*Stachys byzantina*), *Hakonechloa macra* 'Aureola', blue rue, pulmonarias, irises with variegated leaves, a variegated form of *Brunnera macrophylla,* plume poppy (*Macleaya*), *Melianthus major,* variegated forms of miscanthus, dianthus, white-flowered *Achillea decolorans* 'W. B. Child', daylilies (including the long-flowering lemon yellow 'Happy Returns'), *Canna glauca,* gray artemisias, *Phygelius* 'Yellow Trumpet', white-variegated *Phlox* 'Norah Leigh', and such gold-leaved hostas as 'Zounds', 'Gold Edger', and 'Golden Prayers'. This is not a simple composition; on the contrary it is extremely intricate, but the restfulness of the soft grays and pastels and the smooth transitions from one plant or group to the next gives an illusion of simplicity. (Charles Price and Glenn Withey, Seattle, Washington; June)

structure. Books and articles stressing the textural importance of foliage are not lacking but foliage as color has been inadequately covered. Colorful gardens can be created using foliage alone and such gardens involve less labor than those obtaining their effect from flowers. One of the problems in trying to relate color wheel theory to gardening is that, except for green, foliage colors have no place.

Cream, a gentler color than stark white, is also important as a basic color, a fact well known to decorators, who, if undecided or in doubt, paint walls and trim cream or such closely related colors as mushroom and ivory. Cream is none too common among flowers, and it cannot exist alone in foliage, as there must be a proportion of chlorophyll-containing green; branches with all-cream leaves frequently appear on such variegated shrubs as hollies and euonymus and these can be cut off and rooted but the little plants soon die. Cream-variegated foliage may, however, appear predomi-

A vignette from the Price/Withey border, with *Canna glauca, Phygelius* 'Yellow Trumpet', Regal lilies, *Ruta graveolens* 'Jackman's Blue', alstroemerias, *Hakonechloa macra* 'Aureola', and *Artemisia* 'Huntington'. Borders like this are gardening's equivalent of a ballet or symphony, each part complete in itself but all flowing smoothly into the whole.

nantly cream, and such plants are to be treasured. *Sedum alboroseum* 'Mediovariegatum' is one of them. Despite being an herbaceous perennial, it is an attractive presence in the garden for as long as any plant except evergreens. Later I describe and illustrate a border in which this is a keynote echo plant.

Individually or severally, these basic colors fit into almost any color scheme. Note the presence of one or more of them in every scene in this book, and in most other books as well. Though most often used as modifiers or blenders among stronger colors, they can be sufficient unto themselves, as demonstrated in the gray-and-white theme of white gardens. The blender colors hold quiet conversations with each other and serenely beautiful pictures can be composed within this range of colors.

Those who speak loudest and longest aren't more interesting than those of quieter temperament. They usually are more fun and they introduce a note of gaiety to what might otherwise be too solemn a gathering. Quiet and vociferous colors all have their place in gardens, but because they are more versatile, the basic blender colors are given precedence in the following discussion of individual colors.

The echoes concept of limited, coordinated color is the easiest way to ensure harmony. Combinations of closely related colors may not always be the very best that could be done but they will never be eye-shockingly awful. There is, though, the risk of becoming so intrigued with a narrow range of colors that the theme is carried too far. Occasionally, I've felt the need for a strong note of contrasting color. Chartreuse plays a big part in my garden, and in one place golden oregano (*Origanum vulgare* 'Aureum') has spread into extensive sheets. When the garden is rich with other colors, especially the purples most closely associated with it, it seems in proportion, but very early in the year my eye felt the need for a shot of bright color among the expanse of unrelieved chartreuse. It has been achieved by interplanting the oregano with clumps of a little scarlet tulip, *Tulipa maximowiczii*. Only

a few inches high, with narrow leaves proportionately small, it comes and goes in early May, before the purple and lavender flowers get going, leaving behind no messy foliage. Usually, though, introducing more contrast in shape and texture has been sufficient. When looking at the pictures that follow notice that contrast is invariably present, in one way or another.

Green

Being inseparable from most flowers, green is nearly always present whether we will it or not. The most plentiful of all hues, green is as varied as any other color—not one green but many, some dark, some light, some bluish, some yellowish. It is more varied in gardens than in nature because so many of the plants we grow were selected or bred for

A lovely combination of basic blender colors. Plants include a white peony, bearded iris 'White Knight', gray Scotch thistle (*Onopordum acanthium*), blue-gray lyme grass (*Elymus arenarius*), and blue *Nepeta* 'Six Hills Giant'. The purple-leaved smokebush (*Cotinus coggygria* 'Notcutt's Variety') is cut back hard each year to prevent it from growing out of proportion. Spiky *Eremurus stenophyllus* is placed at the back not only because it is tall but because it goes dormant early. The gray foliage to the right is *Epilobium dodonaei,* described by Graham Thomas in the latest edition of *Perennial Garden Plants* as "a beautiful plant in subdued colors, with greyish narrow leaves and long spires of small flowers with purplish calyces." (John Treasure, Burford House, Worcester, England; June)

The leaves of *Selinum tenuifolium* resemble fine green lace. British writer E. A. Bowles thought it the most beautiful of all fern-leaved plants. The umbels of white flowers are equally dainty, resembling those of Queen Anne's lace. Here the foliage overlaps the bold, palmate leaves of *Rodgersia aesculifolia* (England; July)

coloration different from that of the wild population. Most pure stands of conifers, for instance, are a fairly uniform green, but gardeners tend to value more those with blue-green or yellow-green foliage. There are plenty of all-green hostas but in a recent Hosta Society popularity poll, the top twenty were all hybrids and none was a solid green: six were yellow or creamy greens, five were blue-greens, and the rest were variegated with white or yellow.

Greens don't exactly clash, but some are better than others in a given situation: dark green yews make the perfect background for bright colors; a blue-green Lawson's cypress or gray-green juniper would be a good choice for a cool color scheme of pinks and blues and grays, while a golden green Hinoki cypress such as the popular *Chamaecyparis obtusa* 'Crippsii' would be a good choice for a hot color scheme employing scarlet and orange.

Blue-greens, yellow-greens, and variegated greens offer rich pickings for echo purposes and some of these appear elsewhere. Here I am primarily concerned with the calming, unobtrusive green-greens. These usually play second fiddle to the flowers, but, as the pictures will show, green on green

Above
A combination that bright color could scarcely improve. Southern maidenhair fern, *Adiantum capillus-veneris,* has entwined itself with a hosta. They like the same conditions of light shade and soil that does not get dry. (Virginia; May)

Left
There is abundant interest and numerous echoes in this green composition. There are lots of flowers in this garden but the owners lay more store by foliage and are prepared to do the necessary work to prevent the large-leaved butterbur, *Petasites japonicus,* from getting out of control. (Joe Eck and Wayne Winterrowd, Vermont; July)

makes for some lovely cool-looking echoes and provides abundant opportunities for foliar contrast. Combinations I've enjoyed in my own or other gardens include vase-shaped clumps of shuttlecock fern (*Matteuccia struthiopteris*) mixed with lanceleaf hostas (*Hosta lancifolia*) and underplanted with round-leaved wild ginger (*Asarum canadense*); the substantial palmate leaves of a Lenten rose (*Helleborus orientalis*) with the daintier foliage on wiry stems of upside-down-flower (*Vancouveria*), a plant with the grace of maidenhair ferns without their need for abundant moisture; and a green-leaved hosta of unfancy form and medium size with the shining round leaves of European ginger (*Asarum europaeum*) and the airy sweet woodruff (*Galium odoratum*) for contrast.

Green echoes in a scene that makes you feel you could walk right into it, sharing Byron's sentiments: "There is a pleasure in the pathless woods . . . To mingle with the Universe . . ." Nature provides contrast with the shuttlecocks of cinnamon and interrupted ferns rising through a carpet of skunk cabbage (*Symplocarpus foetidus*). All like moist conditions. (Betsy Butzow, New York State; May)

Green flowers can also be grouped in refreshing combinations, with or without additional foliage plants. In one such grouping at Stonecrop I noted feathery ambrosia (*Chenopodium botrys*), lacy gray-green lad's-love (*Artemisia abrotanum*), spires of bells-of-Ireland (*Moluccella laevis*), and the bold leaves and chunky, congested green "roses" of the rose plantain (*Plantago major* 'Rosularis'). One of the pineapple lilies, *Eucomis bicolor*, contrives to echo its broad, arching leaves with an eighteen-inch spike of green starry flowers curiously tipped with clustered bracts in the manner of a pineapple.

Purple Foliage

When I gave a talk called "Making a Pitch for Purple," some of the audience expected it to be about such purple flowers as *Salvia* 'East Friesland', so I'd better make it clear that the color now under discussion is the reddish or purplish brown of such plants as purple barberry (*Berberis thunbergii* 'Atropurpurea') and purple plum (*Prunus ceracifera* 'Thundercloud') and others.

Colors, like clothes, have their fashions, and purple is in vogue among the color conscious. Nurseries are satisfying the demand with an ever-expanding range of plants. *Heuchera* 'Palace Purple' was chosen "plant of the year" by the Perennial Plant Association. I have found this difficult to place, scorching in sun and ineffective in shade. The purple-leaved selections of *H. villosa*, a Southeastern species, are more heat tolerant. *Penstemon digitalis* 'Husker's Red' (an easy, long-lived penstemon with purple leaves) was an overnight success, and so was the oxalis usually sold as *Oxalis regnellii* 'Purpurea' but also as *O. triangularis*. Try using this to echo the purplish veining in the fronds of Japanese painted fern (*Athyrium niponicum* 'Pictum'). *Euphorbia amygdaloides* 'Rubra' quickly gained a place, and the nonhardy *Ipomoea batatas* 'Blackie', a sweet potato selection with leaves so dark they

A hedge of 'Crimson Pygmy' barberry is matched to a purple maple. Simple, and simply perfect. (Allen Haskell, Massachusetts; August)

almost match the name, appears in more gardens every year. As for the celandine (*Ranunculus ficaria*) so appropriately named 'Brazen Hussy', everyone who sees it wants it and given that it increases rapidly I'm puzzled that there doesn't seem to be a commercial source.

New on the scene is *Euphorbia dulcis* 'Chameleon', a bushy mound, twelve to eighteen inches high, with two-inch lance-shaped leaves that are purple most of the time when grown in the sun but sometimes, under the influence of climate, soil, or season, chartreuse or greenish in varying degree. Its stem divides at the tip, these subdivisions terminating in tiny yellow flowers between small, chartreuse-tinted bracts. I'd like to have the foamy chartreuse flowers of an alchemilla pick up this coloring but alchemillas won't grow in sun where I live, so I'm experimenting. One possibility is *Rumex sanguineus,* a sorrel with a pronounced purple vein down the center of its tongue-shaped leaves. If I can find the right sun-shade compromise, *Heuchera* 'Montrose Ruby' is another possibility. This somber group would then be the better for some contrast from brighter color and, risking being trite, I suggest *Coreopsis* 'Moonbeam'. Plants and combinations only become hackneyed when they are good, and there's no better color with purple foliage than pale lemon yellow and no better plant of this color than *Coreopsis* 'Moonbeam'. If you feel you have to be different, try *Oenothera missouriensis* 'Greencourt Lemon', with three-inch bowl-shaped lemon yellow flowers on trailing stems.

Unobtainable still, so far as I know, in the United States, is the first dahlia that won my heart at least thirty years ago, the red-flowered, purple-leaved 'Bishop of Llandaff'. Somewhere I read that this is considered a Typhoid Mary among plants, harboring a virus which it does not itself suffer but which damages other nearby dahlias. I can only say in its defense that in many years of growing it I haven't experienced this problem.

Such edible plants as purple basil, purple lettuce, purple cabbages, and feathery purple fennel are found in flower bor-

ders with increasing frequency, as well as being popular with those vegetable gardeners who have an eye for aesthetics. The purple-leaved grape, *Vitis vinifera* 'Purpurea', used by Miss Jekyll long ago but until recently scarcely available in the United States, is now listed by several nurseries.

Such purple-leaved sedums as Sedum 'Ruby Glow', S. 'Vera Jameson', and S. 'Bertram Anderson' appreciate moister soil than is generally supposed, though not insisting on it, and associate well with the smoky grayish purple of that graceful small willow, *Salix purpurea* 'Nana'.

Old favorites enjoying growing popularity include the little geranium with leaves of bitter chocolate brown, *Geranium sessiliflorum* 'Nigricans' (nice with brown-faced yellow pansies); the small ajuga with crinkled purple leaves known by such varied names as 'Rubra Contorta', 'Metallica Crispa Purpurea', and 'Minicrisp Purple'; purple-leaved cannas; the large-leaved purple plaintain (*Plantago major*

These two plants stood side by side, in containers, at a garden center. By happy chance a branch of the maple's dark wine-red leaves overlapped the golden foliage and carmine buds of *Weigela* 'Rubidor'. (England; June)

107

rubrifolia)—pick off its flower spikes or you'll have seedlings by the million; and the purple-leaved violet long known as *Viola labradorica* but now as *V. riviniana* 'Purpurea' by those able to stay abreast of the taxonomic changes that come so thick and fast. Purple grasses or grasslike plants include purple fountain grass (*Pennisetum setaceum atrosanguineum*), not hardy but clumping up fast enough to be grown as an annual, and black mondo grass (*Ophiopogon planiscapus* 'Nigrescens').

Purple-leaved shrubs include several barberries, with the small *Berberis thunbergii* 'Crimson Pygmy' especially popular. The smaller, more compact *B.t.* 'Bagatelle' would often be a better choice for small gardens but precisely because it is slower growing it is not as often found at garden centers. Purple smokebushes such as *Cotinus coggygria* 'Purple Robe' are popular because they are fast growing, easy to please, and relatively inexpensive. *Weigela florida* 'Foliis Purpureis' (also known as 'Java Red') is a compact form of an adaptable shrub to be found rising among the weeds in many an abandoned or neglected garden. The purple sand cherry (*Prunus* × *cistena*) makes a small tree that could be substituted for its popular parent, *P. cerasifera,* in smaller gardens but what commends it to the color conscious is its willingness to be coppiced into a shrub to be used as a reddish purple moderator in flower beds and borders. Introduced in the United States nearly a century ago and long acclaimed in England, only now is it getting the attention it deserves in the land of its birth.

Purple-leaved maples, on the other hand, are seen in greater numbers and variety in the United States than they are in England, in part because American nurseries first mastered the art of growing them fast to salable size, an achievement aided by abundant warmth and moisture. By contrast, *Rosa glauca* (formerly called *R. rubrifolia*) is seen at its enviable best where the climate has fewer extremes. It does well for me in Virginia, for a while. I'm on my third, earlier plantings having been killed by one or other of the funguses that abound where there is both heat and moisture. The latest purple-leaved entry to be eagerly sought is an elder *Sambucus nigra*

Backlighting renders translucent the large, ribbed leaves of Abyssinian banana (*Ensete ventricosum* 'Maurelii'), revealing the carmine underside. This is matched to the purple maple, which in turn is underplanted with *Heuchera* 'Palace Purple'. The container is also a purplish brown, while contrast comes from the little yellow daisies of *Dyssodia tenuiloba*. (Virginia and Arnie Israelit, Oregon; June)

'Guincho Purple', which has flowers of a particularly pleasing soft, warm pink. At present (June) my youngster planted this year is green. Was it mislabeled? Is it not getting sufficient sun? Pondering this, I got out my *Hillier's Manual*, there to read "leaves green when young becoming deep blackish-purple, red in autumn." We'll see.

Although lumped together as purple-this-and-that, they are a remarkably varied group, and these differences do affect what goes best with what. *Perilla frutescens* 'Crispa', for example, really does look purplish. At Stonecrop, New York, Caroline Burgess used this as backdrop for the wine purple drumstick heads of *Allium sphaerocephalon*. Others are mahogany, brownish, or coppery, some are rich ruby red, some chocolate brown. And to further confuse the issue, some change color during the growing season and the color, or apparent color, of many varies with the strength of the sun and the direction from which it lights the foliage.

Most cultivars of purpleleaf smokebush start the year purplish, becoming redder as the year progresses. In front of one of mine I'd put a daylily called 'Shady Lady', which has light yellow flowers with a dark eye zone. They suit each other when the sun lights them from the front, which it does for part of the day. For a few hours, though, the smokebush is lit from behind. It then takes on decidedly orange tints and a much better echo comes from a vigorous daylily with flowers of dark brick red, acquired under two different names, 'Eric-the-Red' and 'Nashville'. (The same plant, or its twin, is known as 'Stafford' in England.) I recommend it, the flowers being of the older, less voluptuous kind that shrivel neatly, demanding no daily deadheading. Eric and the Shady Lady don't fight, but they do sulk in each other's company, clearly

The dwarf purple osier, *Salix purpurea* 'Nana', has purplish young shoots in spring. Developed leaves are greenish gray but the slender branches have purple bark and this lends a purple haze to this graceful little shrub, emphasized by the adjacent newly emerged foliage of *Lysimachia ciliata* 'Purpurea' and by the wine-red flowers of a columbine, *Aquilegia* 'Double Burgundy'. (My garden; May/June)

110

preferring other companions. What's needed, I think, is a daylily of similar tawny color to 'Eric-the-Red' but with a dark eye zone. Among the thousands of daylilies being purveyed you'd think that easy to find, but the range available to me is much reduced by my preference for those that don't become mush when they die, so I conceived another scheme.

This time my candidate was *Rosa* 'Mutabilis'. This isn't precisely purple, though its young shoots are purplish and young leaves coppery. It isn't precisely anything, instead wearing a coat of many and changing colors, managing this without ever looking gaudy. The effect reminds me of a dancer's or ice-skater's dress consisting of several layers of differently colored tulle, the apparent color changing as the layers move in relationship to each other. Single flowers, graceful as butterflies, start life as orange buds, opening honey-colored, then apricot, then steadily deepening shades of pink, all these colors often present at the same time. All this and gentle fragrance too. And if you ask for yet more, it has few thorns. The perfect echo plant—perhaps the horticultural version of all things to all people?

Alas, the combination, when hatched, proved a disappointment. My affection for the rose is no whit less but the marriage is not a success. As Robert Burns so wryly pointed out: "The best laid schemes o' mice and men, Gang aft a-gley." Of gardeners, too.

Among the best loved purple-leaved plants are those of a soft grayed purple. Two such perennials are *Lysimachia ciliaris* 'Purpurea' and *Sedum* 'Vera Jameson'. Shrubs of this tender coloring include *Salvia officinalis* 'Purpurascens', *Rosa glauca,* and *Salix purpurea,* which is also available in dwarf and weeping forms. If the reason for changing plant names was appropriateness of description, which it isn't, this dainty willow would become *S. glauca.* Its stems are purple but its leaves gray, giving an impression of purple seen through dense fog, ethereal and mysterious. These are pale echoes of the darker purples, sufficiently different to retain their individuality when placed behind or in front of the darker purples, as relative heights dictate. Echoes usually show best when one plant is in front of another, from the commonest angle of view, rather than side by side. A purple smokebush allowed to grow to full height could play foil to *Rosa glauca* placed in front of it, a partnership in which neither constantly dominates. Attention will focus on the rose while it is bearing its small pink flowers, switching later to the smokebush when it produces its seed plumes.

In one way or another, all purple foliage is useful for echo purposes, as well as being valuable as a foil to other colors. At Wave Hill, New York, the artistic and ever venturesome Marco Polo Stufano put together a whole border of purple-leaved plants, highlighted with red verbena. On a smaller scale there are innumerable possibilities, always remembering the need for contrast in size or texture if there is no contrast in color between juxtaposed plants—a bold-leaved canna with the finely cut foliage of purple fennel, for instance, or *Salix purpurea* underplanted with a purple-leaved ajuga. If both have flowers, they must either be in harmony or else come at different times. The flowers could be the basis of further color echoes.

The plants thus far described have purple foliage. There are just a few with flowers of similar dark coloring, be it maroon, deep burgundy, dark crimson, or purple so dark it approaches black. Some fetching low-key echoes with other purples are possible with these: the columbine (*Aquilegia*) called 'Double Burgundy' or 'Double Wine' with *Lysimachia ciliata* 'Purpurea' and *Salix purpurea,* for instance, but by and large these dark colors are better set off by lighter colors, especially gray or amber.

These very dark flowers are eagerly sought by garden colorists and when a new one comes along it is traded first for love, not money, passing rapidly along the plant collectors' chain and soon reaching one of the small plantsman-owned nurseries that are usually first to spot the commercial possibilities of a new plant. A martagon hybrid lily of dark, glossy vinous purple—frustratingly slow of increase—is one

Cirsium rivulare atrosanguineum takes its place in a border of pinks and purples. The plants in the picture are a purpleleaf smokebush, a cotoneaster, and *Geranium endressii*. Other plants in the border include *Weigela florida* 'Foliis Purpureis', purple barberries, *Rosa glauca, Allium schoenoprasum, Euphorbia* 'Chameleon', the purpleleaf filbert (*Corylus maxima* 'Purpurea'), dark crimson *Rosa rugosa, Neillia thibetica* (an unusual shrub, but a good one, with tassels of tubular pink flowers), and the quaint Elijah's tears (*Leycesteria formosa*), with hollow green, bamboolike stems and unshowy white flowers which do, however, draw attention to the claret-colored bracts. (Mr. and Mrs. L. Hattat, Herefordshire, England; June)

that has many drooling with desire, and having seen a small stand of it highlighted against *Rosa rubrifolia,* I've joined the line. There's a clematis I'd like to have added to that combination, *Clematis* 'Purpurea Plena Elegans'. It has little maroon pompons of flower that could echo the more-gray-than-purple foliage of the rose. *Clematis* 'Royal Velours' is another dark beauty, with medium-sized flowers of velvety deep purple.

Daylily, lily, and dahlia catalogues are happy hunting grounds for this sort of color. Most of the dark colors lean toward crimson, purple, or magenta (that's to say that the color contains blue) but *Lilium* 'Beowulf', which I haven't yet seen "in the petal," so to speak, is described as rich, deep blood red. The daylily 'Cape Cod' is a dark wine purple, nicely set off by a group of pink-and-white *Spiraea* 'Shirobana' in the background. I'd like it better if it looked less tawdry when I wander round my garden at 7 A.M., coffee cup in hand, and if removing the offending dead flowers didn't leave me bewailing, like Lady Macbeth, my blood-stained hands—neither red blood nor blue but a color reminiscent of happy childhood hours spent picking blackberries in the hedgerows.

As a bonus to its dark coloring, *Cosmos atrosanguineus* smells of chocolate. The flower is similar in size and shape to that of the familiar annual cosmos. This one is a perennial, not a very hardy one but the root is tuberous and can be lifted and stored, like dahlias, through winter. Hardier perennials include the mourning-widow geranium (*Geranium phaeum*), a maroon-black hollyhock (*Alcea rugosa nigra*), an ornamental burnet (*Sanguisorba tenuifolia purpurea*), which has a basal clump of ferny foliage and five-foot branching stems tipped with thimbles of maroon flowers, *Cirsium rivulare atropurpureum,* with thistlelike flowers of glowing crimson, and a selection of the annual or short-lived perennial sweet william (*Dianthus barbatus*) with purple foliage and flowers of near-black crimson. For a lighter touch there's an annual with a cheerful clownish look, the recently introduced black-and-white-minstrels strain of *Dianthus chinensis,* which has petals of purplish black edged with white.

Knautia macedonica used to be in the genus *Scabiosa* and it still looks like a scabious, with the typical pincushion heads of flower. I've grown it, off and on, for a good many years, and it has always seemed to be a dark, dark crimson. After a few "off" years I recently planted it again and this time the flowers are distinctly purple. A trick of the light? A misidentified plant (I know of nothing similar)? Or does it vary when grown from seed? Just one of those things that keeps garden makers forever on their toes.

Occasionally there comes along a flower that's truly brown. The daylily 'Milk Chocolate' is one such plant. This color doesn't work well against purplish or mahogany foliage. A color that serves it better as an echo background is the light rust or amber of sedges such as *Carex buchananii* and *C. flagellifera,* especially if accompanied by cream or creamy yellow flowers such as those of *Achillea* 'Great Expectations' ('Hoffnung').

Gray

As with other hues, gray is not one color but many. It can be divided into three main groups: the gray grays, the blue-grays, and the silvery grays. The strongly silvery grays draw too much attention to themselves to make good continuity plants. (That job description calls for linking the other plants, not dominating them and stealing the show.) The other grays are outstanding for bringing cohesion to a border, especially when smaller kinds are spaced along the front of a border or used in an unbroken line, none better than *Stachys byzantina* 'Silver Carpet'.

A few grays fit no category. There's a slightly olive-green look to the grayish leaves of *Ballota pseudodictamnus* (a plant more tolerant of muggy weather than most of the gray-felted kinds). The nicest echo I've seen using this came from placing it against a rock dappled with lichens of similar color. Otherwise, the best echoes tend to come from other olive-green foliage rather than from gray. A new ballota called 'All Hallows Green' is more strongly olive, while still retaining some of the grayness.

The gray leaves of a new lamb's ears (*Stachys byzantina*) called 'Primrose Heron' are overlaid with chartreuse and pale yellow and from this, I assumed, came the first part of the name, though I was at a loss to see what there was about it to suggest the long-legged bird I see fishing in the creek outside my bedroom window when I get up in the morning. In fact the name has nothing to do with flowers or birds but commemorates Primrose Heron, mother of Sue Gemmell of Perryhill Nurseries in England, from whom propagating rights to this patented plant can be obtained. It is a most welcome addition to the echoes world because there are so many plants with chartreuse foliage with which it can be

A long-lasting combination of shapes and textures in a town garden. At least five different shades of gray can be counted: the gravel, the container, the dark gray-green of lavender, the medium gray of santolina, and the silver-gray of lamb's ears. The dracaena in the pot and the verbascum in the background add upward thrust and further textural contrast. (George Radford, Victoria, Canada; June)

combined for long-lasting effect—*Hosta* 'Sum and Substance' and golden feverfew (*Chrysanthemum parthenium* 'Aureum') to name just two.

British books will tell you that gray-foliaged plants need full sun, demand perfectly drained soil, and tolerate it dry. And so they do—in England. In Virginia, where I garden now, high summer temperatures and abundant rain result in something akin to a steam bath, which suggests an even greater need for dryish soil, but doing things "by the (English) book" I met my comeuppance with two plants in particular, one of them lamb's ears. The other was *Salvia argentea,* with its great architectural basal rosettes of leaves seemingly clad in silvery mohair. Both repeatedly rotted out. Meantime, a friend living a few miles away was doing well with both. His soil and site were as different from mine as chalk from cheese, mine sandy, his raised beds of rich leaf mold over heavy clay in a small city garden that got more shade than

The wash of lime green over the gray leaves of *Stachys byzantina* 'Primrose Heron' is accentuated by the underplanting of golden oregano (*Origanum vulgare* 'Aureum'). Carrying both colors, it would make a good transition plant between color groupings of gray and chartreuse. (Montrose, Hillsborough, North Carolina; May)

117

Above
A blue-gray grass, *Helictotrichon sempervirens,* plays two roles, echoing the blue cedar (*Cedrus atlantica* 'Glauca') and giving flowing continuity to the bed. Black mondo grass (*Ophiopogon planiscapus* 'Nigrescens'), not an easy plant to use effectively, is well displayed against the gray and gives further flow as well as contrast. (The Scott Arboretum of Swarthmore College, Pennsylvania; August)

Right
In this rock garden, which surrounds a swimming pool, three different shades and textures of gray come from woolly thyme (*Thymus pseudolanuginosus*), lavender, and *Artemisia* 'Powis Castle'. (Polly Rowley, Virginia; September)

Left
A silver willow (*Salix alba 'Sericea'*), trained as a standard, is underplanted with *Artemisia stelleriana*. Both are very cold hardy. (Ellen McFarland, Massachusetts; August)

Below
A gray concrete cat with pea green eyes greets visitors to this garden, a touch of welcoming whimsy that also adds another tone of gray to the planting of woolly thyme, feather-leaved *Tanacetum densum amani,* and a dwarf hebe. (Mr. and Mrs. M. Hughes, Herefordshire, England)

sun. Now I grow both plants in humus-rich, moisture-retentive (but not soggy) soil in places where there's afternoon shade and a temperature often lower by ten degrees or more than it is in full sun.

So if you live where summers are hot enough for hostas to scorch in full sun, you could brighten a shady corner with such yellowy green hostas as 'Sum and Substance' or 'August Moon' combined with *Stachys byzantina* 'Primrose Heron'. For that matter there's many a corner where the outer reaches are bathed by sun all day but the shadowy background only for a few hours, often in late afternoon. Where summers are cool enough for lamb's ears to bask happily in sun all day, golden feverfew would be content in the same quarters.

A plant of somewhat similar coloring, *Helichrysum petiolare* 'Limelight', has a fainter chartreuse tint more evenly diffused over the gray leaves of trailing stems that make it well suited to containers.

White variegations on leaves of green are common. Variegated gray leaves are unusual, so much so that just *having* the rare white-variegated lamb's ears (*Stachys byzantina* 'Striped Phantom') satisfies most, never mind worrying about how best to present it. It can be ordered from Xanadu Nursery (Rt. 3, Box 171, Winslow Road, Williamstown, NJ 08094). *Stachys byzantina* 'Variegata' is the same thing, an invalid name because Latin cultivar names given after 1958 are not permissible under the rules governing botanical nomenclature. An even rarer plant is the white-variegated selection of *Helichrysum petiolare*. Both these have echo possibilities awaiting the attention of the imaginative.

The appearance of grays may change from time to time (sometimes becoming green, for instance, in shade or when wet), but gray leaves are usually opaque—their business is to deflect light, not absorb it. If light does manage to shine through some of the larger grayish leaves, such as those of *Melianthus major,* they appear green. This opacity makes it easier to plan echoes with gray than with the often translucent purple foliage, which may in the course of a day be dark and sultry, glowing wine red, or orange-tinged.

In the absence of variegations, echoes must usually come from gray with gray. I prefer to keep blue-grays and silver-grays a bit apart, basing echoes on differences in shape and texture, or occasionally color when dark gray is paired with light gray. There are so many gray-leaved plants that contriving twosomes is easy. A blue-gray trio I've enjoyed started with *Rudbeckia maxima,* which has clumps of leaves resembling, and rivaling, such hostas as *Hosta sieboldiana.* In front of that went lacy-leaved blue rue (*Ruta graveolens* 'Jackman's Blue'), and in front of that tuffets of *Festuca* sea urchin with its hair-fine blades. This offers both textural contrast and descending height. A blue-gray dianthus could substitute for the blue fescue and I know none better than *Dianthus* 'Inchmery', its pale pink flowers exquisite against its light-reflecting glaucous foliage. These all do well on a slight slope, where water drains away quickly. In a moister, shadier place, a bluish sedge, *Carex glauca,* would make a good partner for any of the large-leaved blue-gray (or blue-green) hostas. The sedge looks better as individual clumps than as the close-knit mat it becomes if not divided every second or third year.

Gray echoes I've noticed in other gardens include *Yucca glauca* (it could be a single clump, or several) rising out of a carpet of woolly thyme (*Thymus pseudolanuginosus*); mounding gray *Santolina chamaecyparissus* underplanted with the lighter gray of mouse-eared chickweed (*Cerastium tomentosum*); the large, silver-plush rosettes of *Salvia argentea* with the cut and curled *Artemisia canescens;* clumps of *Hieracium lanatum*'s gray suede tongues surrounded by the little silver feathers of *Tanacetum densum amani,* and the firmly upright blue-gray form of an ornamental grass, *Panicum virgatum* 'Heavy Metal' underplanted with blue hostas.

White and Cream

The screeching of brakes must be a sound frequently heard as drivers stop without warning to admire this white city garden. Its maker delights in sharing it with neighbors and passersby: the plants "like to be looked at," he says. They include cleome, a white-flowered form of mealycup sage (*Salvia farinacea*), *Cerastium tomentosum,* sweet alyssum (*Lobularia maritima*), a peony, a rose, a white form of coneflower (*Echinacea purpurea*), the large white lily 'Casablanca', *Boltonia* 'Snowbank', a buddleia, white campanulas (*Campanula carpatica* and *C. persicifolia*), anaphalis, irises, *Veronica spicata incana*, white liatris, phlox, astilbe, and dahlia. (Daniel John, Massachusetts; August)

Echoes abound in monochromatic color schemes, of which the "white garden" is one, and the one that has taken the gardening fraternity by storm. In one respect it is a very easy scheme upon which to embark, there being a plentitude of plants with white flowers or gray foliage. There's no such thing, of course, as an all white garden: green or gray is bound to be present in the leaves, usually both. In hot and humid regions, where so many gray-leaved plants don't fare well, it might be better to omit the gray. In practice, white gardens usually contain not only white, gray, and green, but also touches of other pastel colors, especially pale yellows and pale purples. A predominantly white scheme, with touches of blue and pale yellow, can also accommodate some of the peachy pinks that aren't always easy to place.

White flowers are not as simple to unite as one might

A vignette from the same garden, with phlox and mealycup sage echoing the backlit white spots in the leaves of a calla lily.

suppose. At Sissinghurst it is done with a strong and permanent structure of paths and evergreen hedges, within which grows a changing panorama of plants. White borders in other large gardens usually have the benefit of a dark evergreen hedge in the background, to set off the white and hold everything together.

One lesson learned in large gardens is even more applicable to smaller ones: the best flowers for the white garden are not those of spectacular size and pure, glowing whiteness, but those with the softer look that comes from a slight suffusion of some other pigment, usually green or pink, those with a soft and cloudlike look, and those where the flowers are well mixed with green or gray foliage. A few particularly good ones are pink-veined *Geranium clarkei* 'Kashmir White', *Gaura lindheimeri*, Bowman's root (*Gillenia trifoliata*), *Astermoea mongolica* (syn. *Kalimeris*), astrantias, the white form of *Centranthus ruber*, *Crambe cordifolia* (space permitting),

123

This makes the case for simplicity. White narcissus echo the white of the birch tree trunks, with the buildings adding further touches of white. In a partially shady place white foxgloves (*Digitalis purpurea* 'Alba') would also make an echo of dreamy loveliness with white birches. On a smaller scale, white lilies would be beautiful, and they are often fragrant too. *Lilium regale* would be a good choice for sun, *L. martagon* 'Album' for light shade. (John Saladino, Connecticut; May)

Veronicastrum virginicum (invaluable for its graceful spirelike form), and Regal or Madonna lilies. With the softer whites predominating, some of the more eye-catching whites can then be added. Most white-variegated foliage is useful in the white garden, and the ornamental grasses are a group with much to offer, as yet little explored in this context. Three I recommend are the broad-bladed, weeping *Miscanthus sinensis* 'Cabaret', the shimmering, slender-bladed *M.s.* 'Morning Light', and the smaller, more narrowingly upright *Calamagrostis* 'Overdam'. Large-flowered near white daylilies such as 'Joan Senior' are in good proportion with the green-and-white-striped *Miscanthus* 'Cabaret' or the similar 'Cosmopolitan' (they differ in that the edging stripes of 'Cabaret' are green, those of 'Cosmopolitan' white). All the better for our purpose that white daylilies are, as yet, less than a pure and snowy white. The large-flowered white lily 'Casa Blanca' is also excellent.

Because white does not clash with any other color, it

Above
A spring confection of lily-flowered tulip 'White Triumphator' against the white-flowered form of Japanese bleeding heart (*Dicentra spectabilis* 'Alba') (Stonecrop, New York; May)

Left
The white-edged hosta makes a perfect companion for the white azalea, both looking prettier for their association. The hosta is *Hosta undulata* 'Albomarginata', an old one but still the equal of any in garden-worthiness. The touch of blue comes from a self-sown Japanese roof iris (*Iris tectorum*). (My garden; May)

has tended to be thought of as the color to set between two other combative colors. Far from alleviating the problem, putting white between discordant colors only draws attention to your mistake. Cream often does the job better and I wish it was a more plentiful color among flowers.

Thinking of white as a pacifier has caused its role as enlivener to be overlooked. Suppose you've carried out a monochromatic pink theme, with dark pink echoed by medium pink and this in turn by pastels. And now it seems to lack zest. White or cream will give it a lift, especially if the plants chosen are of strong, spiky form. The best plant I know for the purpose is the foxglove, used as single spikes or small groupings spaced unevenly among the other plants. White ones would dominate the planting, elevating the mood as they rocket into space. Cream ones, while still enlivening when placed among darker colors, would be less dominant. White thinly sprinkled throughout will also brighten without being unduly dominant: white larkspur and the white form of *Salvia coccinea* are two possibilities. Both self-sow, and self-sown plants have a way of looking more casual than plants put in place by the gardener's hand, though they may need to be thinned, in their own interests as well as for balance and the well-being of surrounding plants.

Many combinations between individual plants are shown in the photographs so I'll just mention two more from my garden. The first was a bit of intentional color planning, the second lagniappe.

One of two trees (using two was a mistake, one would have been enough) in a fairly small triangular bed is the oriental fringe-tree (*Chionanthus retusus serrulatus*), which in May becomes a cloud of shredded white flowers. Under it grows tough little *Deutzia gracilis,* an uncomplaining shrub through all that the region throws at it of heat, cold, excessive rain, occasional drought, and innumerable pests and diseases. So solid with white flowers are the arching bushes that the foliage cannot be seen. This makes the first echo. Echo two is a bed edging—at least it started as an edging, spreading into a

The very fragrant Oriental hybrid lily 'Casablanca' introduced by B & D Lilies of Washington State in 1987 achieved instant fame. In their catalogue they suggest combining it with the miniature evergreen daylily 'Loving Memories'. I chose to combine it with the broad white-striped blades of *Miscanthus sinensis* 'Cosmopolitan' and a Shasta daisy circulating under several names but most often as 'Becky' (named for Becky Stewart, landscape designer of Decatur, Georgia) and available from Holbrook Farm, NC, under that name. Under whatever name, it is the most heat-resistant Shasta daisy that I have come across. In this same "white" part of my garden there's another lily echo later with late-blooming *Lilium philippinense* against *Miscanthus sinensis* 'Cabaret'. (July)

Right

The white flowers of *Cleome* 'Helen Campbell' hold center stage, with off white *Salvia farinacea* 'Victoria White' in a supporting role, against a backdrop of *Elaeagnus angustifolia,* a large shrub or small tree with silvery leaves. (Denver Botanic Garden, Colorado; September)

Below

An object lesson in perfect placement, the very vigorous silver lace vine (*Polygonum aubertii*) cascades from an entrance arbor, echoing a bank planting of *Euonymus* 'Emerald Gaiety'. The vine can also be enjoyed from a window above. In spring the variegation of the young euonymus leaves is creamy but it becomes white by the time the lace vine flowers. (Susie Russell, Maryland; September)

ground cover, of *Phlox subulata* 'White Delight.' Peak flower for this is a bit earlier but it retains a scattering of white over the green carpet when the other two are in bloom.

The other planting was made for utilitarian reasons. A dogwood was underplanted with *Dentaria diphylla* because little else would grow in the dense summer shade. The dentaria doesn't mind because it goes summer dormant, reemerging in autumn and carpeting the ground through winter and spring. It flowers with the dogwood in April. A dogwood branch, dipping low, layered over the scattered white of the dentaria its own larger blooms.

A dogwood branch, leafless still and dipping low, reveals the white flowers on the underplanting of *Dentaria diphylla*. Soon after the dogwood leafs out, the dentaria will go dormant, reemerging in fall and carpeting the ground through winter. (My garden; April)

Cream is a gentle color, bringing out the best in most other colors but not always combining well with white or silver-gray, which may make it look dingy. Creamy yellow, however, mixes well with both white and cream, so it makes a good transition color between the two. Here *Phlomis russeliana* is growing on higher ground above a bog in which grows a cream-striped grass, *Glyceria aquatica* 'Variegata', and yellow *Iris pseudacorus*. A spear of white foxglove echoes the white of the seat on the other side of the bog. (Mr. and Mrs. M. Hughes, Herefordshire, England; June)

Blue

Blue is a color beloved of poets. "Blue—blue—as if that sky let fall, a flower from its cerulean wall," wrote Bryant, describing the fringed gentian, and "Oh! darkly, deeply, beautifully blue," wrote Byron about the sky, borrowing from Robert Southey, who said it first. Most gardeners share the poets' love of blue; just think what the word "gentian" evokes. How covetable are the blue poppies (*Meconopsis*), and the blue alpine forget-me-nots (*Erytrichium nanum* or *E. aretoides*) are a rock gardener's Holy Grail.

Everyone likes blue but just being blue may not be enough when orchestrating color; its schizophrenic character needs to be recognized. Blue can be as enlivening as spring sunshine or as dampening as a rainy day, varying with the kind of blue, the light, and the other colors associated with it. A blue that sparkles in sun may be moodier in shade, and

130

Nature's echo. The white tips to the blue flowers make bluebonnets (*Lupinus texensis*) particularly vibrant, and they stand out much better against the green of the grass than they would were they solid blue. Echoing both the blue of the sky and the white scudding clouds, they make an exhilarating scene. Theirs is not a moody blue but without the white tips they would look much less lively. (Photograph by Susan Glascock. Texas; April)

blue combined with white or yellow will be livelier than blue combined with green, gray, or purple.

Soft blues and lavenders are tranquil colors, but the relaxation and introspection they induce can become melancholy, summed up in our expression "feeling blue." Great sweeps of blue bring something of the contemplative mood of a Zen garden. Think of bluebells carpeting a wood, whether English (*Hyacinthoides non-scripta,* better known as *Scilla*), Spanish (*H. hispanica*), or Virginia (*Mertensia virginica*). The most recent of such scenes in my mental inventory is a Southeastern woodland garden sheeted in spring with *Phacelia bipinnatifida,* a self-sowing biennial with ferny leaves and circular flowers individually small but carried in such quantity that it forms a sea of misty blue.

I muse that shade does seem to bring out the best in blue, making it more truly blue and creating scenes of haunting, pensive beauty. Then to my mind's eye come more joyous images: of forget-me-nots filling a dry stream and pooling around the trunk of a white birch, of Texas bluebonnets (*Lupinus texensis*) sheeting a meadow with lilting loveliness, of viper's bugloss (*Echium vulgare*) flowing down a Canadian hillside with the vigor of water from a burst dam, and of a cerulean floral reservoir where hardy ageratum (*Eupatorium coelestinum*) had filled a several acre hollow between hills. With scenes of such varied mood in mind, it becomes apparent that blue really does have a split personality, able to gladden, sadden, or induce contemplation.

The variability and changeability of blue were noted by Swinburne when he wrote: "Those eyes the greenest of things blue, the bluest of things grey." Blue may be greenish, or grayish, and its apparent color is affected by adjacent colors, but most blues contain some degree of pink, becoming lavender-blue or violet. These are easy colors to use, mixing well with each other and with other colors. It is the true blues, so eagerly sought, and the rather few greenish blues, that are difficult to fit into monochromatic "blue gardens." Gertrude Jekyll did it (of course). In her studious and classic *Color in Your Garden,* Penelope Hobhouse describes the Jekyll garden and makes other useful suggestions for combining blues.

Not only is blue variable of itself, and made more so by light and other colors, but the palette of blues varies a good deal from one region to another. Many of the purer blues are averse to extremes of heat, or cold, or both, and others to summer drought or humidity and heavy rain. Blue-flowered species of *Ceanothus,* for instance, are just about impossible to grow on the East Coast of the United States, delphiniums don't appreciate hot summers, *Felicia amelloides* and *Convolvulus mauritanicus* (syn. *C. sabatius*) won't survive winter freezes, agapanthuses are only moderately cold hardy, and the exquisite pearly blue *Campanula isophylla* can take neither freezing winters nor sweltering summers.

Never mind, there are others to take their places, including a good many North American natives not yet well known. *Ruellia humilis* is one, a sturdy little perennial charmer with small salvers of clear, soft blue. Deep-rooted, drought-resistant, and entirely self-sufficient, it self-sows in hot, sunny places, inveigling itself among other plants without overwhelming them. The taller, deeper blue *R. strepens* is just as willing—a bit too generous with its progeny in fact, but definitely worth considering for a poor, dry place where little else will grow. Let me not gloss over their shortcomings though. They start their day early, then from early afternoon, when they've done their stint for the day, one must rest content in the expectation of more tomorrow . . . and tomorrow . . . and tomorrow. The friend who gave me my first ruellia called it "breakfast flower," presumably because that's the time of day when it is at its best. No deadheading is needed and the plants never look scruffy.

The attractive blue-green foliage of the adaptable, pest-free *Baptisia australis* would earn it a place even if it never flowered. That place, however, tends to be a larger one than many gardens can spare. *B. minor* is less than half its size. One of the best additions to my garden in many a year, the flowers ape blue lupines and the foliage is exquisitely lacy. At the time of writing, Woodlanders in Aiken, South Carolina, is the most likely source for this. Some interesting hybrids of intermediate size are also turning up, so keep an eye on baptisia listings in the plant catalogues. Darker blue cultivars of Siberian iris such as 'Dewful' make good echo marriages with blue baptisias.

Lobelia siphilitica has been somewhat overshadowed by its brilliant relative the cardinal flower (*L. cardinalis*). It is easier to grow and lovely in its own right, if a bit overendowed with green foliage. *Salvia azurea* is one of the clearest, most cerulean blues, its brilliance accentuated by neat, graygreen foliage. Its habit, alas, is not neat. To be frank, it flops. When you garden in a hot climate, much is forgiven a plant that comes through summer as uncomplainingly as this one does, but in my garden staking is not acceptable, so I let it

There's matching color but contrast in flower size and form from *Baptisia australis* and Siberian iris 'Dewful'. (Andre Viette Farm & Nursery, Virginia; June)

Right
This combination of globe thistle (*Echinops*) with lavender demonstrates repetition of color with contrast in form. (Hestercombe, a restored Jekyll garden, Somerset, England; August)

Below
The flattish heads of *Verbena* 'Lavender' seem poised over a blue cloud of *Calamintha nepeta*, grown from seed labeled "blue form." In moist soils and warm climates verbenas spread very fast and this one has to be cut back from time to time to prevent it from engulfing the calamint. (My garden; September)

sprawl as it chooses. Subsidiary stems from the main ones then turn themselves upright and it makes as pretty a late summer picture as anyone could wish.

And then there are the amsonias. Years ago I read some words that stung. The Japanese, the writer suggested, exported only the clumsiest and most garish flowers, being under the impression that all foreigners had bad taste! Join those refuting this by making greater use of the amsonias. Each and every one is welcome in my garden. If it had to be just one, I'd be hard pressed to choose between *Amsonia montana* (syn. *A. tabernaemontana* var *montana*) and *A. hubrectii,* the first for its compact size, the second for its fine-cut foliage and amber autumnal color. True they don't flower for long but they grace their place with good foliage all through the growing season and ask so little in return. Their soft, pearly or grayed blue fits in anywhere and lends itself well to echoes with the darker blue of many Siberian irises. Amsonias are clumping plants that seldom need dividing. Their Oriental cousin, amsonia orientalis (*Rhazya orientalis*), bears similar flowers, less abundantly but for longer, on a spreading plant. I don't rate it as highly but in some regions it may be better; trying them is the only way to find out.

Among the purest blues are those of the wild commelinas, but there's too little flower in proportion to leaf and lanky stem, so they get pulled out as weeds. Look for seed of *Commelina tuberosa*—if, that is, you are there in the morning to appreciate flowers bluer than the skies in travel brochures; they are gone, alas, by early afternoon. Once you have this, it may self-sow, or the tuberous roots can be lifted and stored through winter.

Adaptable, available non-native plants of a good blue include *Brunnera macrophylla* for early flowers and blue plumbago (*Ceratostigma plumbaginoides*) for late ones. In my garden taller *C. willmottianum* is also a reliable late bloomer but it probably wouldn't survive north of the Mason-Dixon line. Technically a shrub, it is killed to the ground in winter, re-emerging fairly late in spring. Both these blue plumbagos can

'Summer Skies' is the fitting name for this dainty Siberian iris with white falls and standards of soft cerulean blue. *Amsonia tabernaemontana* repeats the blue. (My garden; May)

135

be underplanted with small, early bulbs. Then there are irises, blue flaxes (the commonest of these, *Linum perenne,* is native to western North America, the less often seen *L. narbonense* to Europe) and several veronicas ('Sunny Border Blue' is the best I've grown). The South American *Salvia guaranitica,* an intense dark blue, remains a presence in the garden until hard frost, at which time, where the ground freezes, its tuberous roots can be lifted and stored.

The genus *Dracocephalum* includes some good blue plants and one of these, *D. rupestre,* was a partner in my own blue "echo of the year." The dracocephalum is a lax, low-growing plant with neat dark green foliage and dragonhead flowers of deep cornflower blue held on branched foot-high stems, continuing through most of May in my garden and probably for longer in cooler regions. The dracocephalum's flower stems lolled over its neighbor, *Pratia pedunculata* (often sold as *Isotoma* or *Laurentia fluviatilis* in the United States). This creeping plant hugs the ground in a mat of tiny leaves, becoming a pool of baby blue when it bears its constellation of tiny starry flowers in spring and early summer. In a moist, sunny place it romps away: "Mary's-menace" and "Roxie's-revenge" are two of the more repeatable names I've heard applied by rock gardeners to plants of such rapid spread. Only little alpine gems are at risk from the pratia; among shrubs and robust perennials it does no harm. It is not very cold hardy and in my coastal Virginia garden most of it dies when we get a colder than average winter. A fragment usually survives to make a comeback. Unlike most plants, which incline toward the strongest light, the dracocephalum stems spread out radially. Not only, therefore, is it echoed by the pratia, but it contrasts prettily with the creamy foliage of three other plants: *Hosta* 'Shade Fanfare' is to its left, and *Liriope muscari* 'Variegata' mingles with *Sedum alboroseum* 'Mediovariegatum' behind.

Available species of blue-flowered shrubs aren't numerous but what they lack in quantity they make up for in variability of size, foliage, and blueness within each species.

Hydrangeas, caryopteris, and buddleias are among the most useful. The latest caryopteris introduction is *Caryopteris* × *clandonensis* 'Worcester Gold', instantly popular because the golden green foliage extends its season of interest and sets off the blue flowers extremely well. I sought a blue-flowered low-growing perennial to place in front of this. Asters flower at the same time and I settled on 'Professor Kippenburg'. And here was the story of blue in a nutshell. It wasn't bad—blue is never awful—but it wasn't quite right either. Distance might have deceived the eye into thinking them a good match but in juxtaposition they were neither alike nor sufficiently different for a successful echo. The next step will be to grow several likely asters in a nursery bed and compare colors at

The violet-blue of lavender is matched to the rich purplish blue flowers of potato vine (*Solanum crispum*) trained on the wall in the background. The purple tint of the potato vine is repeated in the pinkish purple carpeting thyme. Tussocks of a blue-gray fescue (*Festuca*) grow in front of the lavender. (Goodnestone Park, Kent, England; July)

flowering time. Blue is a particularly difficult color to select from memory, pictures, or descriptions.

The most widely grown of all blue-flowered shrubs is lavender, especially 'Hidcote Blue'. Where this does well it is a good choice for edging borders and tying mixed colors together, but the blue contains some pink and is in poor accord with pure or greenish blues.

If the soil is sufficiently acid and the climate sufficiently mild, there are some beautiful blues among the many cultivars of *Hydrangea macrophylla,* both mophead and lacecap kinds. They vary a great deal, innately or under the influence of soil and light. The color being less dense, lacecaps such as 'Blue Wave' are better mixers than the mopheads. Their blueness, or lack of it, can be a cause of exasperation. Change anything around them and their color may change: some of mine showed their gratitude for a topdressing of rich (brought in) topsoil by turning—not pink, I wouldn't have minded that

The violet-blue of *Geranium* × *magnificum* is picked up in the sepals of a seedling columbine. The white petals of the columbine provide contrast, and the yellow stamens link it to the adjacent yellow columbines. (Margaret Lockett, Seattle, Washington; June)

so much—a muddy mixture of nothing-in-particular colors. A dressing of sulfur usually puts things right but this instability makes them poor echo candidates. Hydrangeas used to be hard to find, but Winterthur Gardens in Winterthur, Delaware, now offers a nice selection called 'Blue Billow', and the mail-order nursery Heronswood in Kingston, Washington, has a big selection, including my personal favorite, the fairly compact 'Ayesha', usually described as pink but a beautiful clear blue in acid soil. It is not as cold hardy as 'Blue Billow'.

There are quite a lot of clematis with flowers of violet-blue or indigo (a color defined in the old Royal Horticultural Society Color Charts as "Union Jack blue") and these, grown on trellises, tripods, or such other support as you can devise, extend echo possibilities in small gardens by utilizing vertical space. In one garden I saw 'Ramona'—one of the handful available at most garden centers—growing on a wall trellis, with the foundation bed below filled with dark blue columbines. Most blue columbines are violet-blue. The Rocky Mountain columbine, *Aquilegia caerulea,* comes nearest to true blue of those I've grown, and because it has both blue and white in the flower it makes a very good echo plant. One of the purer blue clematis is 'Perl d'Azur'. The trailing, non-climbing *Clematis* × *durandii* is a glowing indigo blue, and my mind made the connection with *Salvia* 'Indigo Spires'. The color combination wasn't bad but *S. guaranitica* is better. Furthermore, it stands firmly upright, while 'Indigo Spires', unless staked or pinched, flops about and smothers everything within its extensive circle.

One of the best clematis combinations I've seen was at Goodnestone Park, England, in July, where a clematis with small, light blue nodding flowers (I don't know which one it was but 'Betty Corning' would do) was intermingled with the larger, dark purple flowers of *Clematis* 'Etoile Violette'. There's nothing clematis like better as support than their own stems or those of another clematis, so this combination made practical sense as well as being aesthetically pleasing.

Although the old adage "blue and green should never be seen" is not nowadays heeded by the fashion world, often the best thing green does for blue flowers is stay out of their light, with foliage minimal in proportion to flower, or confined to basal clumps as in delphiniums.

Greenish blue (turquoise) is a vibrant color, with no hint of melancholy. It mixes poorly with the pinkish blues. There aren't many flowers of this color but one of my hydrangeas (name unknown) comes close, a wonderful brightener for summer shade when there's no competing color. Blue butterfly weed (*Oxypetalum caeruleum*) is another. Blue poppies lean in that direction, and so does love-in-a-mist, *Nigella damascena* (for mixing with the lavender-blues, try the less common *N. hispanica*). Yellow flowers—pale or lemony, not brassy—are lovely with turquoise: blue poppies with yellow primroses, for example, or with *Hosta fortunei* 'Aurea' which, when newly emerged, is of an almost ghostlike pale butter yellow.

"Blue gardens" are difficult to compose. Echo groups of two or three plants are easy, provided there's contrast of some kind and that blues on the green side of pure blue aren't combined with blues on the violet side.

Chartreuse and Golden Greens

The greeny yellows and yellowy greens known variously as chartreuse, lime green, pea green, or sulfur are a varied group, some leaning more toward green, others more toward yellow. On the RHS Color Chart the last patch in one of these groups is called chartreuse-yellow and the first patch in the adjoining group is called chartreuse-green. At the extreme of yellowness, foliage is usually described as golden, or yellow, but something of green is always present, the green tints usually becoming more dominant in shade, the yellow ones usually less so as the season progresses but sometimes the reverse: the golden barberry (*Berberis thunbergii* 'Aurea') changes from vivid yellow to lime green, for instance, while creeping charlie (*Lysimachia nummularia* 'Aurea') becomes so brightly yellow by blooming time that the yellow flowers are almost invisible against the foliage. The yellowy greens and the greeny yellows mix together quite well but when chartreuse is combined with another color, its exact tone can make the difference between a good effect and a perfect one: use the yellower tints with hot yellows, oranges, and scarlets, the greener tints with lavenders, violets, and purples.

Green is a quiet color, yellow a conspicuous one. These in between colors offer something of the best of both worlds: the blendability of green and the excitement of yellow. Chartreuse mixes well without either overwhelming its companions or becoming subordinate to them. Hence the popularity of *Alchemilla mollis,* one of the most widely used of all perennials.

Plants are plentiful in this range of colors, primarily from foliage but also from flowers, at least if one regards the bracts of numerous euphorbias as "flowers" in this context. *Euphorbia palustris* with chartreuse-leaved or yellow-variegated hostas is one good combination. Many of the foliage plants are variegated, and many are evergreen conifers, with their lasting structure and year-round appeal. And these colors can be found in plants of just about every shape and size, from such prostrate carpeters as Scotch moss (*Sagina subulata* 'Aurea'), to such popular small trees as the golden honey locust (*Gleditsia triacanthos* 'Sunburst') and the yellow-leaved robinia (*Robinia pseudoacacia* 'Frisia'). This breadth of choice makes "golden gardens" second only in popularity to white ones among monochromatic themes.

Conifers, with their needlelike foliage, lend themselves perfectly to facing down with bold-leaved hostas, but sun and shade requirements must be kept in mind. This differs from region to region and from plant to plant. Soil also makes a difference; plants can stand more sun if it is rich and moist. In general, conifers color best in sun and hostas prefer light

Above and right
Even on overcast or rainy days this golden garden seems bathed in sunlight. A laburnum is in bloom but most of the color comes from foliage plants, especially evergreen conifers. Golden thyme fills the crevices of the paving square. Plants have been thoughtfully combined to contrast in texture or form. Clumpy hostas and columnar conifers flank the seat. Behind it is a golden Pfitzer juniper. (Crathes Castle, Scotland; June)

142

shade, but it is often possible to find a compromise and some hostas are more sunproof than others. Planting hostas on the shady east or north-facing sides of the conifer is one possibility, but the yellow coloring of the conifer will be less intense on that side, and sometimes entirely green. Such fine details of placement call for on-site observation of patterns of light and shade. If you need help selecting hostas, visit the gardens of hosta enthusiasts in your area (you can locate them by joining the Hosta Society) to find out which cultivars are known to do well. Golden hostas could grow through a lawn-like ground cover of Scotch moss for an "all-gold" combination. If there's shade and moisture enough to manage this combination, you might like the addition of *Smyrnium perfoliatum,* an English wildling biennial with parsleylike heads of greeny yellow flowers on two- to three-foot stems threaded through leaves of the same coloration. If it likes the site it will self-sow. If you like chartreuse with blue-green (some do, some don't), blue-leaved hostas could be added to break up the yellowy mass. On the sunny side of the conifer you could have *Euphorbia myrsinites,* with its glaucous foliage and greeny yellow bracts.

There are innumerable other possibilities for the sunny side of conifers. Leave a gap, though, on every side, for all but the carpeters, otherwise you risk shading to death some of the conifer foliage, and nothing looks more conspicuously disfigured in the barer winter scene than a conifer with dead or missing sections.

New plants come along every year. One of my most successful ground covers for sun is golden oregano (*Origanum vulgare* 'Aureum'). There's a bit too much green in this to make it a good companion for my two favorite golden conifers, the goldthread cypress (*Chamaecyparis pisifera* 'Filifera Aurea') and one of the Japanese Hinoki cypresses (*Chamaecyparis obtusa* 'Crippsii'). The golden oregano grown in English gardens, which I now believe to be *Origanum vulgare* 'Iet-swaart', is a more golden green, but it is less robust and soon died out during summer's heat and humidity. Now there's a

Golden oregano (*Origanum vulgare* 'Aureum') echoes *Hosta fortunei* 'Albopicta'. (Crathes Castle, Scotland; June)

143

new one that seems to combine the vigor of one with the golden green of the other. Called 'Norton's Gold', and thought to be a hybrid, mine came from Canyon Creek Nursery in California. It hasn't flowered yet, but I'm told the flowers are pink. If you'd rather have blue flowers, try *Veronica prostrata* 'Trehane', a low-growing plant with leaves very like those of golden oregano and flowers of brilliant blue.

Liriope muscari doesn't survive extreme cold but it can take hot sun. The ubiquity of *L.m.* 'Variegata', with chartreuse stripes becoming cream, testifies to its adaptability. *L.m.* 'Pee Dee Ingot' (available from Powell's Nursery, Princeton, NC) is a newcomer with short, neat leaf blades that are golden in full sun, lime green in shade. The flowers are lavender-blue.

In a corner near my goldthread cypress there's a greeny yellow columbine I visit often—giving it every chance to win me over! When there are visitors with me I pause here, without comment, and await their reaction. In general it tends to

The reds, oranges, and bright yellows of tulips, pansies, and basket-of-gold (*Aurinia saxatilis*) supplement the golden greens in this yellow garden. Plants with golden green foliage include golden privet (*Ligustrum ovalifolium* 'Aureum'), golden barberry (*Berberis thunbergii* 'Aurea'), golden honey locust (*Gleditsia* 'Sunburst'), and golden creeping charlie (*Lysimachia nummularia* 'Aurea'). (Ladew Topiary Gardens, Maryland; May)

be of the "Am I supposed to like this?" kind, but there's at least one eager adoptee if it finally gets the thumbs down. It has two names, *Aquilegia vulgaris* 'Variegata' and *A.v.* 'Aurea', and therein lies the rub. I bought it based on a description of bright golden foliage and flowers of milky white to pale purple. Of the three plants I bought, one has golden leaves and has not yet flowered, and the other two have green leaves with the sort of viruslike wiggly yellow streaking unpleasingly reminiscent of leaf-miner damage. The flowers are light purplish pink. If you like this sort of thing, it combines well with the feathery leaves of golden feverfew (*Chrysanthemum parthenium* 'Aureum'). If you don't, perhaps weeding out variegated seedlings would refine the strain.

There are numerous ivies that could ramble around the base of a golden conifer to create an echo. If you like speckled and spotted things, try *Hedera helix* 'Luzii', which is green marbled with light greenish yellow. The wavy-edged leaves of *H.h.* 'Lemon Swirl' are predominantly creamy green when

Greeny yellows in this picture include three shrubs: a golden form of ninebark (*Physocarpus opulifolius*) in the background, *Lonicera nitida* 'Baggesen's Gold' to the left, and *Spiraea* 'Gold Flame' to the right. There's chartreuse from the alchemilla at the base of the sundial, and the orange azalea is underplanted with Bowles' golden grass (*Milium effusum* 'Aureum'). (Mrs. Arnold Rakusen, England; June)

young, becoming greener at maturity. New growth is made from spring through fall, so there's always a good proportion of creamy leaves. *H.h.* 'Gold Heart' has triangular, shallowly lobed leaves with green edges and bright yellow centers. *H.h.* 'Buttercup' is bright yellow in sun but pale green in shade.

Keep an eye on ivies, though. Unlike most plants, they travel toward shade, not sun, and if you are not alert they'll be climbing the conifer. An occasional wandering strand will do no harm, but let them rip and they'll smother the conifer. In any case, echoes aren't effective when the colors are so similar and the plants so closely intertwined. Better to aim at contrast, using vines, perhaps annuals, with small or sparse foliage. Red or scarlet flowers are especially showy against golden green foliage. One vine always remarked on in British gardens is a climbing nasturtium, *Tropaeolum tuberosum,* with flowers that look like flights of tiny scarlet swallows. Few North American gardeners can grow it; it doesn't even survive the coldest zone 8 winters. My substitute in Virginia is the firecracker vine, *Manettia cordifolia.* This hails from South America and is usually considered a zone 8 plant but it has been in my garden some fifteen years, surviving along the way a run of winters more like the average zone 6. It climbs by thread-fine stems clad in tiny leaves and bears flights of little scarlet trumpets all through summer. The flowers of *Eccremocarpus scaber* are somewhat similar, resembling small scarlet goldfish with wide open yellow mouths. This is a tender perennial, often grown as an annual.

At the foot of my goldthread cypress I put out each year one of nature's showiest creations, the glory vine (*Gloriosa rothschildiana*), sinking it in the ground still in its pot. Its tubers, intriguingly shaped like little white boomerangs, increase quite rapidly. It makes lax stems about two feet long in the course of a season, attaching itself by curling leaftips to any slender means of support. In my garden it flowers for only two or three weeks, in early summer, but what a show, while it lasts, from the large, spidery red-and-yellow flowers. It is stored in a frost-free place through winter. When nonhardy

plants are put out this way, sooner or later one forgets, or just can't be bothered, to bring them in for winter. That, usually, is that, but sometimes one discovers that the plant is hardier than generally supposed. Glory vine survives the average winter in my garden but not the coldest ones, making it of similar hardiness to dahlias but less hardy than cannas.

With simple combinations of two or three plants, it is hard to know where to begin, so great is the scope, greater in fact than in any other color. Hostas might make the best starting point. There are hundreds to choose from: yellow leaves broadly or narrowly, evenly or unevenly edged green, or green leaves similarly edged yellow, leaves with yellow streakings and marblings, leaves of solid yellow, big leaves and small ones, smooth or wavy, rounded or strap-shaped. Look through an illustrated hosta book and you'll find you are spoiled for choice and there's a big risk of overuse. Hostas cry out for companions other than their fellow hostas. Most

White is the secondary theme in this golden garden. The central row of *Spiraea* 'Gold Mound' is flanked by rows of white-flowered *Daphne caucasica,* which repeat the white of the seats, paintwork, and container flowers. The yellow-leaved forsythia is one of a pair placed on either side of the Japanese lantern. Set back from this, out of the picture, is another white-painted seat flanked with golden mock oranges (*Philadelphus coronarius* 'Aureus'), and a pair of white-painted birdhouses rise among a green background of screening shrubs. (Ellen McFarland, Massachusetts; August)

hostas have broad, uncut leaves, so narrow or ferny ones give good textural contrast. I know of only one gold-variegated fern, and that one, *Arachniodes simplicior* (also known as *A. aristata* 'Variegata'), is rather slow growing and therefore hard to come by, but there are many yellow or yellow-striped grasses or grasslike plants, none better, where hardy, than the popular and inexpensive *Liriope muscari* 'Variegata'.

Popular golden grasses include Bowles' golden grass (*Milium effusum* 'Aureum'), Bowles' golden sedge (*Carex elata* 'Aurea'), *Hakonechloa macra* 'Aureola', and a showy gold-striped sedge, *Acorus gramineus* 'Ogon'. Where space is limited, seek out the tiny *A. g. minimus* 'Aureus'. Its narrow, bright gold leaf blades are seldom as much as six inches long and because they are held in fans angled at thirty degrees, the height is half as much. A triple echo in my garden combines this with two other plants of very different texture; a bold-leaved clump of *Hosta montana* 'Aureomarginata' is at the back and in front of it is a tiny-leaved, fine-textured shrubby

Lonicera nitida 'Baggesen's Gold' behind the seat is counterbalanced by the golden bamboo (*Arundinaria viridistriata*) on the left. Golden creeping charlie wanders over the paving. (Kathleen Hudson, England; July)

honeysuckle, *Lonicera nitida* 'Baggesen's Gold', faced down with several clumps of the tiny golden sedge.

Some readers will, I'm sure, question the use of the honeysuckle in this context. Its color and fine texture have long made it a popular evergreen in English gardens, where it forms a three- to five-foot bush and often takes its place in sunny borders, as I assume it also does in the Pacific Northwest. It lingered for years in my garden, looking pitiful and never more than six inches high—good years, too, without summer drought or excessive winter cold. Tried and found wanting, I was ready to chuck it out but on the suggestion of a friend gave it one last chance in shade, to which it responded with immediate gratitude. Now fifteen inches high, an annual clipping will maintain it at that. This species responds well to clipping and in England is often used for hedging. A friend in Pennsylvania tells me that winter takes care of the pruning there—it survives but at ground-cover level. Do grow it if you can; I know of no other golden green plant of similar textural quality.

Prime among flowering plants with chartreuse flowers (or bracts) is the big range of euphorbias. *Nicotiana alata* 'Lime Green' is an annual tobacco plant with flowers of the familiar size, while *N. langsdorfii* is a charmer with smaller, dangling flowers of similar color.

If you seek more suggestions for combinations, here are a few I've enjoyed, in my own or other gardens: Bowles' golden sedge with *Euonymus* 'Emerald 'n' Gold'; *Acorus gramineus* 'Ogon' arching over an underplanting of *Hedera helix* 'Luzii'; gold-leaved *Hosta* 'Aurora' growing through golden creeping charlie (*Lysimachia nummularia* 'Aurea'); the sulfur-yellow flowers of rue (*Ruta graveolens*) matched to an underplanting of golden oregano (*Origanum vulgare* 'Aureum'), spiced up by a crimson-purple rose on the fence behind; creamy chrysanthemums with a greeny yellow eye in front of a chartreuse-leaved privet (*Ligustrum* 'Vicaryi'), then underplanted with *Lonicera japonica* 'Aureoreticulata', a honeysuckle with gold-netted leaves; the end of a wall with a yellow Pfitzer juniper on one side and *Euonymus* 'Emerald 'n' Gold' climbing it on the other; *Lonicera nitida* 'Baggesen's Gold' giving emphasis to the greenish yellow banding in the upright blades of *Miscanthus sinensis* 'Strictus'; the long strands of *Geranium* 'Ann Folkard', with its yellowish leaves and magenta flowers, trailing over *Hosta* 'August Moon'; *Alchemilla mollis* with the yellow-variegated rue, *Ruta graveolens* 'Icterina'.

At Stonecrop, New York, in a mostly shady place beneath tall trees an arching clump of *Hakonechloa macra* 'Aureola', with chartreuse-striped grassy blades, was combined with chartreuse-flowered *Patrinia gibbosa,* a plant not often seen but a worthy one. Writing in *Perennial Garden Plants,* Graham Thomas describes it thus: "A strange plant. The long-lasting flowers, beautiful still when faded, are small, but with one long petal of sharp greenish yellow. They appear in massed array over broad basal leaves. For part shade or at least a cool root-run. It gives the effect of a coarser *Alchemilla mollis* late in the season. The flowers give off a horrid whiff of dogs; dog-lovers please note."

Chrysanthemum pacificum, with silvery edges to its leaves, is primarily a foliage plant. Where summers are long, it opens little tufts of bright yellow flowers in November but its best time is October, when the chartreuse buds, as round and polished as ball bearings, glisten and gleam in the bright light of an Indian summer. A superb companion for it then is golden feverfew (*Chrysanthemum parthenium* 'Aureum'), with feathery leaves that are chartreuse until autumn, becoming a brighter gold through winter where the climate is mild enough for it to persist. A chartreuse-fruited nandina could go behind this combination. Both these chrysanthemums have now been put in different genera but I'm retaining the familiar names until the dust (or ruffled feathers) from recent changes in nomenclature settles. The best way I know for home gardeners to keep abreast of the name changes that come so thick and fast is to buy *The Plant Finder* available from the British Hardy Plant Society and from some sister societies in the United States.

Left
Euphorbia epithymoides is matched to a golden hop (*Humulus lupulus* 'Aureus'). Later a climbing pea aptly named *Lathyrus chlorantha* 'Lemonade' will wend its way among the yellow leaves of the hop. (Stonecrop, New York; June)

Below
The sulfur-yellow flowers of *Euphorbia sequierana niciciana* echo the color of *Hakonechloa macra* 'Aureola', while its fine foliage provides contrast. Where summers are hot, the hakonechloa needs moist soil and shade from afternoon sun. (Barbara Flynn, Seattle, Washington; June)

Above
Golden Scotch moss (*Sagina subulata* 'Aurea') is a good filler for paving crevices but in hot regions it needs shade. Lady's mantle (*Alchemilla mollis*) trails over the edge of the path. There's color contrast from the purple thyme that also grows in the paving. This short stretch of path connects the driveway with a lawn. (Louise Kappus, Ontario, Canada; July)

Right
The seed heads of many plants take on greenish tints. Here the mop heads of *Hydrangea arborescens* 'Annabelle' match the pale chartreuse bands in the leaf blades of *Miscanthus sinensis* 'Zebrinus'. (Nan Sinton, Massachusetts; August)

Left
There's a double echo here: the pink columbines match the pink flowers of *Weigela florida* 'Variegata', while the greeny yellow flowers of *Euphorbia characias* echo the foliage of shrubs which include *Elaeagnus pungens* 'Maculata', a golden holly, and a gold-variegated euonymus. In cool regions the variegation in the leaves of the weigela is also greenish yellow at this time of year; in hotter ones it starts off cream. (Doris Willmott, England; June)

Below
The leaves of the full-moon maple (long called *Acer japonicum* 'Aureum' but now *A. shirasawanum* 'Aureum') scorch in hot sun but lose much of their color in deep shade. Happy here in dappled shade, it is underplanted with golden hostas and Bowles' golden grass (*Milium effusum* 'Aureum'). (Charles Price and Glenn Withey, Seattle, Washington; June)

The colors discussed so far are minglers, easy to mix with each other and with other colors. Now we come to the showier colors, those capable of devolving into a color maelstrom if randomly mixed together, with pairs among them capable of shrieking at each other.

Yellow

April echoes and reflections from daffodils, forsythia, and the golden twigs of a weeping willow. (Richard and Alice Angino, Harrisburg, Pennsylvania; April)

Some theorists define yellow as a "hot" color, to be grouped with orange and red in lively color schemes. Others define it as a "cool" color, to be grouped with blue and green. It is both. Sandwiched as it is between its fellow primaries, blue and red, yellow has only a small center point of pure yellow-

ness before it slides, as in a tug-of-war, in one direction or the other. The yellow sometimes called "canary" is close to the center point. From there it either moves toward red, becoming a warmer golden (or brassy, depending on your predilections) yellow, or toward blue, becoming cooler and eventually greenish. With achilleas, for example, 'Moonshine' and the newer 'Anthea' are clear, bright yellows, while 'Coronation Gold' and 'Gold Plate' are warmer yellows. As between two daylilies of similar dainty, self-cleaning flower form, 'Corky' is a clear lemony yellow, 'Golden Chimes' a warm one. It does neither of them justice to put them side by side.

The clear yellows mix less well with warm colors than with cool ones. The cool, lemony yellows mix better with pinks and lavenders than the warm yellows do. Bright yellow flowers can be appealingly echoed with a paler yellow, but even with pastels just any yellow won't do. *Anthemis tinctoria* 'Wargrave', for example, is a soft, pale yellow, but still a warm one, whereas the pale yellow of *Coreopsis* 'Moonbeam' is cool. If you sought echo companions for these among the sunflowers (*Helianthus* and *Heliopsis*), the lemony yellow *Helianthus* 'Capenoch Star' would pair well with *Coreopsis* 'Moonbeam', and *Anthemis* 'Wargrave' with the warmer yellow of most of the others.

Unexpected or unlikely echoes bring another pleasurable element to gardens—surprise. In England's Hidcote Garden I admired such a combination of two seemingly incompatible plants. A santolina with creamy yellow flowers (possibly 'Edward Bowles') hung over the edge of a pool, echoing the flowers of a pale yellow waterlily just below.

Monochromatic schemes encompassing both warm and cool yellows are seldom satisfactory if the two are mixed together, but warm yellows could be used at one end of a border, cool yellows at the other, bridged by cream or creamy yellow.

Orchestrating plants is a continuing process of appraisal and reevaluation. Inevitably, some experiments fail. Ghastly

A sequence of yellows is interspersed with scarlet. Bearded iris 'Sahara' in the foreground is underplanted with the yellow-and-white annual *Limnanthes douglasii*. Then comes *Achillea* 'Coronation Gold', then *Aquilegia formosa,* and finally the yellow rose 'Helen Knight' on the house wall. (Sissinghurst, England; June)

Right
Although the flowers of *Solidago* 'Golden Mosa' and *Anthemis* 'Grallach Gold' are similar in color, contrast is provided by their very different shapes and textures. Notice the use of the word "gold" in both names, indicating warm yellow. Even with such strong textural contrast, these two would not combine nearly so well if the anthemis was lemon yellow. (England; August)

Below
Because they are difficult to propagate, the yellow and white variegated forms of *Aralia elata* are costly. They are, nonetheless, eagerly sought. They are large shrubs or small trees. This one is A.e. 'Aurea Variegata', combined with a dainty daylily called 'Tetrina's Daughter'. *Campanula lactiflora* can be seen on the left. (Charles Price and Glenn Withey, Seattle, Washington; June)

combinations aren't a problem, they are ripped out with celerity. It is those that fall just short of anticipated beauty that bring a nagging discontent, the mental equivalent of poking a sore tooth, wondering whether it can be fixed or whether it should be pulled. This is balanced by elation when a combination looks as good in the ground as it did in the mind's eye. Four echoes in one of my borders gave daily pleasure for many weeks at various stages of the long season.

The border faces west, backed by a hedge of *Photinia* × *fraseri*. The bright coppery new growth of the photinia called for care in choosing colors to go in front of it. Yellows in the range from clear yellow through sulfur, lime green, and cream became the theme colors, with blue as a secondary color and minor notes of gray, white, and pink—pale pink, in the main but also, for verve, the bright, clear pink of *Verbena* 'Silver Anne' at ground level, where it isn't seen in conjunction with the coppery orange new growth toward the top of the background photinias.

When you see the same plant in garden after garden, in many parts of the country and in combination with many different plants, you know that it is versatile and reliable. *Miscanthus sinensis* 'Zebrinus' is one such plant. Striped leaves are common, banded ones unusual, which helps make this one of the best-selling grasses. The three tall, yellow-flowered perennials with which it is combined are cupflower or rosinweed (*Silphium perfoliatum*), wild senna (*Cassia marilandica*), and *Rudbeckia nitida* 'Herbstsonne'. A golden conifer is just visible on the right. (Sheila McGullion, Massachusetts; August)

Yellow flowers include daylilies, *Oenothera tetragona* 'Sonnenwende' ('Summer Solstice'), which has purple young foliage, *Anthemis* 'Creamy' (sulfur-yellow until the flowers fade to cream), a canna with creamy green venations in its leaves and yellow flowers (possibly 'Nirvana'), *Coreopsis* 'Moonbeam', a lemony yellow hollyhock (*Althaea rugosa*), the bushy, glaucous-leaved *Hypericum frondosum, Helianthus* 'Capenoch Star', *Helenium* 'Kugelsonne' ('Sun Sphere'), a very late bright yellow button chrysanthemum, and, flowering nonstop from June to frost, a double form of the annual *Portulaca oleracea.* Unlike those with single flowers, this stays open all day. I value it highly and keep it going under lights through winter.

One of the echoes that pleased me so much, the combination of a blue verbena and calamint, is pictured on page 134. Other blue flowers include asters, the self-sowing biennial viper's bugloss (*Echium vulgare*), violet-blue Japanese irises grown from seed, asters, *Amsonia montana,* early

Small though it is, the little bit of yellow from an evening primrose in the left corner of the steps balances the composition by echoing the yellow corydalis on the other side. Put a finger over it and see what a difference it makes. Creeping thyme and *Dianthus deltoides,* some planted, some self-sown, fill crevices in steps and paving. (Patrick Lima and John Scanlan, Larkwhistle Garden, Ontario, Canada; July)

Left

There's a double echo here. The gray foliage of *Thalictrum speciosissimum* matches the gray leaves of a Scotch thistle (*Onopordum acanthium*) in the background, while the bicolored torch lily (*Kniphofia*) both echoes and contrasts with the thalictrum flowers. (Glyndebourne, Sussex, England; July)

Below

Plants, left to right, include: *Artemisia* 'Powis Castle', *Phalaris arundinacea* 'Feesey's Variety', *Boltonia* 'Snowbank', double yellow *Portulaca oleracea, Aster* 'Professor Kippenburg', *Anthemis* 'Rebecca Broyles', canna (*Achillea* 'Creamy' next to the canna has flowered and been cut back), *Verbena* 'Lavender' with *Calamintha nepeta, Rosa roxburghii, R.* 'Mary Rose', *Verbena* 'Silver Anne', and portulaca. *Aster caroliniana,* not shown, is just to the right. (My garden; October)

Left to right: *Canna* (possibly 'Nirvana'), *Achillea* 'Creamy' (which will be cut back hard after flowering), *Anthemis* 'Rebecca Broyles', *Rosa* 'Mary Rose', *Verbena* 'Lavender'. (Early June)

blue-and-yellow Dutch irises, hyssop (*Hyssopus officinalis*), and the very late-flowering, brilliant blue *Ceratostigma willmottianum*. There's also pink from two roses, the pale pink English rose 'Mary Rose' and the double-flowered chestnut rose, so called for its burry buds, *Rosa roxburghii*. Engulfing the remains of *Cotinus* 'Grace' (graceless, dead, and not mourned) is one of the Southeast's great gifts to gardeners, the climbing aster (*Aster carolinianus*), weeping down like a bride's train and smothering itself in autumn with small aster flowers of a color that seems bluish in the evening and on dull days and at other times somewhere between lavender and lilac. One plant to be seen in the pictures—not bad but not a planned part of the color composition—is *Echinacea*

160

purpurea. It got there because that was the only gap I could find at the time.

Another satisfying echo combined the daylily 'Icecap', which is almost white with a lime-green throat, with the chartreuse foliage of *Caryopteris* 'Worcester Gold'. The daylily flowers for about two weeks. Immediately in front of the caryopteris is *Amsonia montana,* its blue flowers echoed in spring by the blue and pale yellow bicolor flowers of Dutch irises interplanted with the daylilies, and in front of the amsonia blue asters make a marriage with the blue fall flowers of the caryopteris. Two other echoes from this border are shown in the following pictures.

Repeatedly one must ask: "Is this the very best plant for the purpose?" Because the answer was "yes" last year, it doesn't follow that it still is. For one thing, proportions change as plants mature and this may call for reassessment. For another, after decades of the doldrums, today's gardeners are living through America's horticultural renaissance, with the country second to none in the introduction of new plants. One of these is *Anthemis tinctoria* 'Rebecca Broyles', named for the gardener who found it. This was one component in a satisfying echo with the canna. If cut back when it gets lanky, the anthemis goes on producing its clear yellow flowers all summer. But there is more. The ferny foliage is marbled with creamy green, very showy early in the year, before the flowers hide it, and a perfect match for the veining in the canna leaves, with the sulfur yellow flowers of *Achillea* 'Creamy' making an echo trio. Some new plants work out less well. An artemisia with foliage patterned in cream, acquired as *Artemisia indica* 'Variegata', proved to be one of the most invasive plants I've ever grown, far worse than *Artemisia* 'Silver King'. Be warned.

Plants present are: Canna, *Anthemis* 'Rebecca Broyles' (flowering for a second time after being cut back), *Panicum virgatum* 'Heavy Metal', *Echinacea purpurea,* and *Helianthus* 'Capenoch Star'. (October)

Red, Scarlet, Orange, and Golden Yellow

A single touch of red adds drama to a planting and, with the possible exception of red-and-purple borders, a little red is usually better than a lot, which limits its echo possibilities. Outside tropical regions, red flowers are a scarce commodity anyway, which explains the ubiquity, where they are hardy, of the few available flowers of what the RHS Color Chart calls Guardsman's red, notably *Crocosmia* 'Lucifer', *Dahlia* 'Bishop of Llandaff', and some poppies. Poppies are too fleeting to make good echo subjects, dahlia catalogues and display gardens are a better place to look; dahlias flower for a long time and there are quite a lot of good reds among them. Their flowers being so different in form, red dahlias combine well with *Crocosmia* 'Lucifer', and also with the spires of *Lobelia cardinalis*.

Green is red's complementary color, and complimentary too. Nowhere is red more showily itself than amidst an expanse of green. One of the most rewarding plants in a lightly shaded part of my garden is the painted arum, *Arum italicum* 'Pictum', which has arrow-shaped leaves patterned in silvery white. They emerge in autumn and remain through spring,

There's a pleasing but short-lived echo from *Potentilla atrosanguinea* and an Oriental poppy. When the poppy goes summer dormant, the lax, branching stems of the potentilla will help fill the gap. (Jane Platt's garden, Oregon; June)

Above
The red fruit spikes of *Arum italicum* 'Pictum' rise up through ferns and hellebores to enliven shade. There's a background echo, not shown in the picture, from the late blooming, scarlet-flowered *Rhododendron prunifolium*. (My garden; July/August)

Left
Lantana camara 'Spreading Sunset' and *Tagetes patula* 'Espano Granada' make a well-matched pair for a sunny place. Although similar in size and color, the flowers are sufficiently distinct to retain their individuality. (Longwood Gardens, Pennsylvania; July)

repeating the white in the swordlike white-edged leaves of a *Rohdea japonica* cultivar and, in spring, the white flowers of *Dicentra spectabilis* 'Alba'. After the arum leaves have died away, up through the lacy fronds of the tassel fern (*Polystichum polyblepharum*) and texturally contrasting palmate leaves of hellebores, rise stalks of glowing scarlet fruits to echo the scarlet flowers of *Rhododendron prunifolium,* a late-blooming, deciduous species, in the background.

Many plant nurseries have extensive display beds such as this to demonstrate ways of using the plants they sell. Echoes abound among the extensive range of plants in this hot-color border. Plants include *Verbascum nigrum,* a horned poppy (*Glaucium corniculatum*), achilleas, dianthus, *Crocosmia* 'Lucifer', *Heuchera* 'Palace Purple', *Agastache coccinea, Phygelius* 'African Queen', *Gaillardia* 'Burgundy', *Oenothera odorata* 'Sulphurea' (an evening primrose that starts off palest primrose yellow and fades to tints of apricot and pink), *Monarda* 'Cambridge Scarlet', and the shrubby *Hypericum androsaemum,* which has small yellow flowers followed by showy red-and-yellow fruits. (Mary and Leah Fisher, Cultus Bay Nursery, Whidbey Island, Washington; June)

As increasing increments of yellow pigment are added to red, it becomes first scarlet and then orange. These, with the golden yellows that contain a soupçon of red, are the "warm" colors. If a border of warm colors is to be at its most lively, chartreuse-yellow is the best foliage color to add. In the other direction red moves through crimson, purple, and violet toward blue. Gray and purple are good foliage colors to use with these cooler reds and pinks. Reds are easiest to work with if one keeps to one side or the other but if scarlets are to be combined with crimson, then purple foliage and such dark burgundy flowers as *Achillea* 'The Beacon', *Gaillardia* 'Burgundy', and *Dianthus* 'King of the Blacks' will ease the transition, as will such flowers as *Hemerocallis* 'Palace Guard', which combines dark crimson with copper and warm yellow in its flowers.

Scarlet is a fiery color and it burns its brightest when mixed with oranges and golden yellows in "hot" color

This is one of the echo components in the Fisher border. *Achillea* 'Paprika' makes echoes of its own as the dark pink buds open to flowers that become progressively paler as they mature. *Dianthus* 'King of the Blacks' matches the darkest stage of the achillea's coloration.

Arrangements by Leah Fisher and ten-year-old Brita Fisher, using the flowers picked from the border shown. In the well-chosen copper jug Brita has used orange alstroemeria, yellow verbascum, the poppylike dark apricot horned poppy, *Agastache coccinea,* bronze fennel, *Gaillardia* 'Goblin', *Achillea* 'Paprika', an orange-scarlet honeysuckle (*Lonicera* 'Dropmore Scarlet'), *Phygelius* 'African Queen', and *Dianthus* 'King of the Blacks'.

In the basket Leah used many of the same flowers and also *Gaillardia* 'Burgundy', *Hypericum androsaemum, Macleaya cordata,* yellow *Primula florindae, Achillea* 'Salmon Beauty', *Solidago* 'Angel Wings', a potentilla, *Buddleia* 'Empire Blue', and, in the center, *Aster × alpellus* 'Triumph'.

schemes, but the relative density of a color also influences the way it is perceived. In one of my borders where pink is the main theme, the scarlet sage, *Salvia coccinea,* sows itself around. It flowers continuously and prolifically for months but the individual flowers are small and the color thinly spread, so the effect is a red haze that is never overwhelming, seldom disruptive, and more at home in this border than in another employing hot colors. The pink border terminates in a large dogwood (*Cornus florida*), which puts on a berry display in autumn of similarly scattered color. An unplanned echo occurred when the salvia (which, in the Southeast, is at its best in autumn) sowed itself in front of the dogwood.

Orange is often considered a harsh color, and it can be, but notwithstanding widespread distaste for this hue, orange geums sell in very large numbers, especially *Geum ×* 'Borisii'. This flowers in unison with *Euphorbia griffithii* 'Fireglow' and the two could be echo-mates in the spring or early summer garden, perhaps with blue-leaved hostas or blue forget-me-nots. Blue is orange's complementary color. The brilliant blue found, for instance, in *Delphinium grandiflorum* would make a partnership of considerable impact. The blue of forget-me-nots or blue hosta leaves makes for gentler contrast. If you opt for forget-me-nots, try the perennial water forget-me-not, *Myosotis scorpioides*. Glossy-leaved and flowering all summer, as well as being long-lived, it is superior to the better known annual or biennial *M. sylvatica*. In the wild the water forget-me-not grows at the edge of ponds and streams and it does prefer moist soil though it need not be soggy. *Geum* × 'Borisii' also likes moist soil and, in hot regions, a little shade; when hot and dry it becomes a target for red spider.

Many flowers that are predominantly orange also have touches of pink in their petals. Orange with pink is a com-

In this lightly shaded part of my garden emphasis is on foliage. Color is secondary but spring is welcomed in with a bright splash of scarlet. The matched pair of shrubs in the foreground are *Spiraea japonica* 'Golden Princess'. (May)

Evergreen Japanese azaleas 'Stewartsonianum' are echoed by the scarlet of *Geum* 'Red Wings' and scarlet-and-yellow columbines (*Aquilegia canadensis*). The gray-green on the left is *Sedum* 'Autumn Joy'. The feathery leaves are Queen Anne's lace (*Daucus carota*), which must have been present as seed in topsoil added in autumn as a surface dressing; although unplanned, it was an attractive addition for both foliage and flower. (May)

bination many profess to dislike, but nature frequently puts them together to charming effect. There was no disharmony in a grouping at the Scott Arboretum consisting of a snapdragon called 'Longshot Orange', which is pink in bud, opening to bright apricot, *Dahlia* 'Autumn Leaves', with petals of pale apricot shading to deep pink centers, and *Agastache* 'Apricot Sunrise', which speaks for itself.

Those who abhor orange are usually thinking of the color found in marigolds, butterfly weed—and oranges, of course! At the softer end of the orange range come some of the most exquisite and romantic of all colors, from salmon and pastel coral to orange-buff and amber and bronze. Look to daylilies for lucious fruit salad colors of apricot, melon, or peach. Colors aren't limited to this range but include, by means of throats or eyebands of different color, such fanciful concoctions as melon with raspberry and pineapple, or peach with plum and banana. Like mixed fruits in cream, they all

168

Hosta 'Golden Tiara' echoes golden lemon balm (*Melissa officinalis* 'Allgold'). Between them a green-bladed form of *Carex buchananii* is just starting to make its new foliage. Between this and the hosta there's a very early dwarf daffodil, *Narcissus* 'Little Gem', which holds the stage in February and disappears from sight when the hosta emerges from its winter rest. Between the carex and the lemon balm a die-back shrub, *Hypericum moderianum* 'Tricolor', is just starting into growth. When it is fully grown, its slender branches arch out and mingle with the sedge. The pink edge of the leaves is echoed by a double-flowered impatiens. This combination remains effective until hard frost, which is seldom before November. (May through October)

blend together, and prettily, but oh, what a waste of individual beauty. For all the popularity of daylilies, rare indeed is the garden where flowers of singular beauty are removed from the chorus line and given the entourage that enables them to star. It must, I am convinced, be done on the spot, so tiny, but so important are differences in color.

As I write I'm feeling a bit smug, having just united in marriage (Mormon-style!) a crimson-banded salmon daylily acquired under the name "red-eye," which has flowers of the modest size I prefer, with *Achillea* 'Salmon Beauty' and the cinnamon-bladed *Carex flagellifera.* Another plant in this bed, *Agastache* 'Firebird', compensates for the loss of several Cape fuchsias (*Phygelius*), which thrive for me only in partial shade and even there are nothing to boast about. *Agastache* 'Firebird', on the other hand, takes in its stride all that summer brings, keeping up its airy display of small orange tubular flowers on loosely bushy, small-leaved plants well into autumn. Bolder foliage is provided by a compact canna called 'Pfitzer Chinese Coral'. This too keeps on going and going and going, joined in autumn by the massed bloom from two chrysanthemums: single-flowered 'Apricot' is indeed apricot in bud, becoming silvery pink, and 'Bronze Elegance' has tightly packed pompons of a soft orange-tan. A bit farther along colors become a more golden apricot to buff with *Agastache* 'Apricot Sunrise' and one of the David Austin English roses, 'English Garden', with slightly fragrant "old-fashioned" double flowers of a warm buff-yellow tinted apricot at the center. The English roses get leggier in warm regions of the United States than they do in England but 'English Garden' is more compact than most. There are several in this delectable range with apricot or coppery orange tints in their flowers, including 'Sweet Juliet', 'Apricot Nectar', and the patio rose 'Sweet Dream'. Patio roses fall midway between miniatures and floribundas in size and appearance, making them a good choice for smaller gardens. I find them very tempting but there's probably more than enough in this bed already and instead of adding more I should increase the quantity of some plants there already. Lured by a plethora of plants and combinations they long to try, the color conscious, no less than plant collectors, can spoil the effect by cramming in too many different things.

Blue is the secondary color in this bed, from the early *Salvia urticifolia* and *Nepeta nervosa*, long-flowering *Boltonia latisquama* 'Nana', midseason *Aster laevis,* and the very late *Aster oblongifolius* 'Raydon's Favorite' (available from Holbrook Farm, Fletcher, NC).

Crimsons and Pinks

The rose has been called "the queen of flowers" and pink is the commonest color among roses, so for as long as the rose reigns supreme, beds and borders based on pink are likely to outnumber other color schemes. Does the baby clothes fashion of "pink for a girl, blue for a boy" get imprinted on our minds? Pink and blue is the most popular garden color scheme and a great many men name blue as their favorite color.

From the center point of pure red, with scarlet on its other side, colors move through crimson, purple, and violet toward blue, and these, with their paler tints and darker shades, make a harmonious range. Pink is derived from red diluted with white or gray. A few pink flowers might be called pale red, or pale crimson—clear pinks containing little or no blue—*Rosa* 'Betty Prior', for instance, or *Verbena* 'Silver Anne', a very good echo pair, but most pinks contain some blue. All these consort harmoniously with the lilacs, lavenders, purples, and violet-blues in color schemes that seldom go badly awry.

Only the handful of yellowed or coral pinks look uneasy among the clear or blued pinks. Recently I put out close together a number of seed-raised sweet williams (*Dianthus barbatus*). When they flowered, all but one were within the blued pink range from crimson to purple. The exception was

Right
Most plantings of azaleas welcome spring with the flower power of scarlets, yellows, and bright pinks. Here, for a change, is a combination of pastel pinks from Exbury azalea 'Irene Koster' underplanted with the slightly paler *Geranium macrorrhizum* 'Ingwersen's Variety'. (Susan Ryley, Victoria, Canada; May)

Below
Flower arrangements are borders in microcosm and arrangers have a big advantage when they grow their own flowers. Purplish pink is the theme for this arrangement of *Perilla frutescens* 'Crispa', zinnias, cosmos, and amaranthus. (Lib Ferebee, Virginia; September)

Above
A dark-flowered form of Lenten rose (*Helleborus orientalis*), seen through the yellow-barked branches of *Cornus stolonifera* 'Flaviramea', is echoed by the pale pink flowers of *Lamium maculatum* 'Roseum'. It is easy to see how the lamium in this picture could be added to the combination in the picture on the left. (Montrose, Hillsborough, North Carolina; April)

Left
Helleborus orientalis abchasicus is an exact color match for the buds of *Daphne odora,* with a paler pink echo from the opened flowers of the daphne. Because they come when the weather is cool, the daphne's flowers last for two or three weeks if not spoiled by frost. The hellebore flowers start earlier and continue for many weeks. (My garden; March)

a coral pink resembling one sold as 'Newport Pink'. "Which is the odd man out?" I asked visitors ranging from an artist friend to an eight year old unlikely to have developed a sophisticated color sense. All, without hesitation, picked out the coral pink. There's a trap for the inexperienced among colors that shift as the flowers mature, sliding from blued pink into the red-orange range. *Sedum* 'Autumn Joy' is such a plant. When the flowers first open it fits well with the pinks, but when its color matures to salmon-bronze, it will be at odds with them. Suitable companions for this invaluable plant include grasses, autumn-flowering blue asters and monkshoods (*Aconitum*), creamy spired *Sanguisorba canadensis,* and many chrysanthemums with 'Bronze Elegance' especially good.

A dusky pansy (possibly 'Arkwright Ruby') is combined with the paler, dusty pink of *Phuopsis stylosa.* (Sissinghurst, England; June)

Above
Here's a summer-long combination of self-sufficient plants, spotted looking after themselves on the grounds of a holiday cottage. The gaunt, lichened stems of an old, unpruned *Rosa rugosa* provide support for the perennial pea, *Lathyrus latifolius,* which supports itself by tendrils. It flowers all summer and autumn and is evergreen in mild climates. (French Farm House, Whidbey Island, Washington; Late June)

Left
Allium schoenoprasum 'Forescate', seen behind *Geranium sanguineum* 'John Elsley', has both ornamental and culinary value. A vigorous form of chives, if a portion of its leaves are removed for kitchen use, it will quickly replace them. (My garden; May)

There are numerous echoes in this border of glowing pinks interspersed with blues, violets, and purples, with continuity provided by gray foliage along the front and purple perilla further back. Among the plants in flower are several kinds of *Phlox paniculata* including 'Starfire', 'Tenor', and 'Franz Schubert', *Cleome* 'Violet Queen', *Gaillardia* 'Burgundy', ruby red snapdragons, perovskia, *Monarda* 'Blue Stocking', *Salvia* 'Indigo Spires', *Salvia* 'East Friesland', platycodons, *Verbena bonariensis,* and *Veronica spicata*. Siberian irises 'White Swirl' and 'Caesar's Brother' and *Baptisia australis* bloomed earlier. *Aster* 'Alma Potschke' and *Sedum* 'Autumn Joy' are still to come. Gray foliage includes lamb's ears (*Stachys byzantina*), grassy *Helictotrichon sempervirens,* and artemisias. (Elsa Bakalar, Massachusetts; August)

By and large, pink flowers are easy to fit into the garden. Only when bright pink is combined with orange (a combination best avoided by the color timid) is the result sometimes cacophonous. There's a risk that romantic combinations of pale pinks, blues, lavenders, white, and gray will look insipid, especially in bright sunshine. Adding lemon yellow cuts the sugary effect.

If a pink-blue scheme still seems wishy-washy, it needs

the stronger pinks, and with these come abundant opportunities for echoes between soft pinks and brighter ones, perhaps including such strong magentas as *Geranium psilostemon, G. sanguineum,* and the purple loosestrifes (*Lythrum salicaria*). A soft pink astilbe such as 'Cattleya' makes the perfect partner for *L. s.* 'Morden's Pink'. The lythrum goes on flowering much longer than the astilbe, so add a pale pink bee balm such as *Monarda* 'Croftway Pink' to keep the softening echo going a bit longer.

I felt the need for a splash of brighter color in a part of my garden where Polly Hill's Choptank azaleas—deciduous, very fragrant shrubs with running roots—wander around a large-leaved hybrid rhododendron called 'County of York'. The proportions are maintained by cutting the azaleas back hard when they get much more than two feet tall. Their starry flowers are white with long pink tubes, while the much more substantial trusses of 'County of York' are pink in bud, opening to white. It is a pretty combination but green was the only other color present here in spring, a time of year when gardeners hunger for color. It was given a lift with an evergreen azalea called 'Rose Glow'—a much brighter pink than the name suggests. One was enough, as the bright pink might otherwise have overwhelmed the more delicate colors.

My own perceptions of color are often considerably different from color chart definitions. In the intense summer heat and sandy soil of my garden, many hybrid coralbells (*Heuchera × brizoides*) have failed to prosper but two from Nancy Goodwin, called 'Shere Variety' and 'Unimproved', have done very well. If you'd asked me I'd have said that these and the plants combined with them leaned toward coral pink, but when I checked the heucheras against the RHS Color Chart they turned out to be two-tone currant red. Currant red is a midrange red, before it veers toward scarlet in one direction and crimson in the other.

Heuchera 'Unimproved' combines nicely with *Lonicera × heckrottii*'s crimson tube and banana yellow interior. This is a vining honeysuckle, but by dint of frequent cutting back

Part of the Bakalar border, with an annual nicotiana matched to *Monarda* 'Colrain Red', globe thistle (*Echinops ritro*), purple coneflower (*Echinacea purpurea*), *Artemisia stellerana,* perovskia, *Liatris* 'Kobold', purple heliotrope (*Heliotropium arborescens*), and purple perilla (*Perilla frutescens* 'Crispa').

Right
This and the following pictures are from a border in my garden where pink is the primary color. The pictures on pages 30 and 31 are also part of this border. *Rosa* 'Betty Prior' flowers until hard frost. It is echoed, fairly briefly, by the dianthus sold in the United States as 'Bat's Double Red', which isn't red at all. The blue in front of it is *Veronica* 'Goodness Grows', capable of growing much taller but staying low in this sandy soil. The green foliage at the bottom is *Phlox subulata* 'Scarlet Flame'. (May)

Below
Phlox subulata 'Scarlet Flame' is interplanted with pink tulips. This year it is 'Angelique', delicately flushed bright pink to repeat the pink of the phlox. (April)

Left
Clematis 'Mme. Julia Correvon' clambers through *Rosa* 'Petite Pink'. The rose not only supplies support but it shades and protects the roots of the clematis. The rose flowers only once, and not for long, so this combination is of fairly short duration. (May)

Below
Salvia vanhouttei seldom survives winter even in zone 8 but cuttings root easily and grow fast when set out in spring. The flowers are closed broad beaks of velvety garnet, with a glimmering of brighter color as they open to reveal scarlet throats, reminding me at this stage of the clamoring mouths of baby birds demanding to be fed. Its echo companion is *Chrysanthemum* 'Mei Kyo', one of the best for the Southeast. It is very hardy but it flowers too late where autumns are short. (November)

of wandering strands I maintain it as a free-flowing bush of mounded habit. *Heuchera* 'Shere Variety' is combined, in a shadier spot, with a small azalea called 'Balsaminaeflora', which has flowers like little rosebuds, and with the fringed flowers of a hybrid between two native catchflies, the pale pink *Silene polypetala* and the red *S. virginica.* The color checked out as carmine, which is closer to crimson than coral, while that of the azalea is described as "claret rose," scarcely a helpful description, and quite unlike any claret I've seen. These are set against a backdrop of a taller azalea called 'Hampton Beauty', which isn't bad but one of slightly warmer pink called 'Fashion' would be better. *Fragaria* 'Pink Panda', with strawberry-type flowers of a somewhat paler tint than the silene, also wanders around. The point I'm trying to make is that these colors, which were worked out on the spot, echo each other very well, but I'd never have thought so if I'd planned it "by the book."

A color-coded notebook of combinations seen and admired is a useful memory jog and kindler of ideas when planning new beds or refurbishing the old ones. These are a few pink combinations I've noted: 'Corsica' lilies underplanted with *Coreopsis rosea* in front of the shrubby *Spiraea japonica* 'Shibori' ('Shirobana'), which has flat, lacy heads of flowers tricolored in white, pale pink, and deep pink; *Cleome* 'Rose Queen' with clear pink buds matching *Aster* 'Alma Potschke', with the cleomes' opened flowers providing a paler echo; 'The Fairy' rose intermingled or faced down with such magenta flowers as *Lythrum salicaria,* petunias, or *Geranium sanguineum* for a contrasting color echo, or with *Heuchera* 'Chatterbox' for an echo of matching color, contrasting form; a group of Asiatic lilies in blending pinks ('Cherished', 'Corsica', 'Crete', 'Malta', and 'Unique') among mixed astilbes in a similar pink blend; pale pink *Lespedeza thunbergii* 'Pink Fountain' cascading over the much brighter pink of *Aster* 'Crimson Brocade'; soft pink *Boltonia* 'Pink Beauty' in the center of an island bed, with the clear bright cerise-red of *Aster* 'Alma Potschke' in front of it as seen from one side, and *Salvia greggii,* of similar

bright pink, on the other side; *Cosmos* 'Sea Shells', in pale and deeper pinks, echoing both the pale pink *Boltonia* 'Pink Beauty' and the bright pink *Aster* 'Alma Potschke'.

Purple Flowers

Purples and pinks mix well together but purple, or purple-violet, is at its most vibrant with its complementary color, yellow. When the colors are at full strength, this is a strong dose of color, as it also is when purple flowers are combined

One English wildflower book describes fumitory (*Fumaria officinalis*) as a "widespread and plentiful weed," which should not discourage the use of this pretty clambering annual in gardens. The varied tints of pink in the flowers make it an excellent echo subject. It has no visible means of support but will hitch itself up through a shrub to a height of about three feet. Here it is combined with the tall, lax shrub rose 'Cerise Bouquet' and magenta *Geranium psilostemon*, speared by the leaves of deep violet-blue *Iris sibirica* 'Tropic Night', which flowered earlier. (Charles Price and Glenn Withey, Seattle, Washington; July)

Above
The dark purple stripes in the flowers
of the mallow, set on a paler tint, form
an echo complete in itself. It is then
tossed in with pink and blue larkspur
for an easy-care cottage garden
grouping. (Polly Munz, New York
State; July)

Right
Campanula latiloba 'Hidcote Amethyst'
is echoed in the slightly paler tints of
annual candytuft (*Iberis umbellata*).
(Margaret Lockett, Seattle; July)

with chartreuse foliage. *Salvia* × *superba* 'East Friesland' and
Achillea 'Coronation Gold' or 'Parker's Variety' would make
a striking accent in a border but a whole border devoted to
such strong color would be overwhelming. Cream, creamy
or pale lemon yellow, gray, and pastel purple mingle more
quietly and could be the basis for a larger planting.

All or any of these can also act as modifiers for strong
purple, as they do in one of my plantings based on yellows
and purples. *Malva sylvestris* 'Mauritiana', a biennial or short-
lived perennial mallow with flowers which, at first glance,
appear to be solid purple, though in fact they have very dark
purple veining on a slightly lighter background, makes a good
echo partner for its sibling *M.s.* 'Zebrinus', which has stripes
of matching purple on a pale purple background. These stolid
bushes, dense with flowers, are made less weighty by the
gray leaves and pale lilac flowers of a mint (*Mentha longifolia*)
that wanders around and between their feet, having escaped
the prescribed limits of its sunken plastic pot. In front of these
is *Marrubium cyllenium,* a horehound grown mostly for its
gray-green woolly leaves but briefly doing its bit toward
color echoes with bobbles of pale purple flowers widely
spaced along its upright stems. Pastel purple *Monarda fistulosa*
in the background may or may not participate—one year it
attended the party, the next it came too late. Across the path
the pale purple color is repeated in low-growing patches of
Verbena tenuisecta 'Edith'. Other flowers in this bed are yellow.
A practical afternote: the torrential rain of a thunderstorm
toppled the heavy mallows in midperformance so, such
storms being the norm where I live, they'll play no part in
my future plantings.

Farther along, in light shade, evergreen azaleas called
'Misty Plum' are banked at the foot of a pine which supports
Rosa 'Veilchenblau', a thornless multiflora rose with bunches
of lilac-purple pompon flowers. The path in front of the azaleas is informally edged—not, that is, in rows but in a casual
wander-as-it-will sort of way, with a dwarf mondo grass
(*Ophiopogon*) having arching blades striped in cream and

What appears to be a massed display of purple tulips is in fact a well-thought-out blend of two kinds, 'Insurpassable' and the deeper purple 'The Bishop'. (Nemours, Delaware; May)

green. Other plants here include the vivid purple hardy orchid, *Bletilla striata,* the chartreuse-yellow *Hosta* 'August Moon', and the low-growing cream-variegated, yellow-flowered *Sedum lineare* 'Variegatum'. The rose shares its tree with a clematis which is, if I recall correctly (the label has long since been lost), a purple one. In many years there have been no flowers to jog my memory—too much shade it seems. Clematis do vary in the amount of sun they need. I'll have to find a more shade tolerant kind.

Bletilla striata does so well in my garden that I've now planted it through an ivy with creamy yellow young leaves (*Hedera helix* 'Lemon Swirl') in front of an evergreen azalea called 'Koromo Shikibu', with strap-petaled flowers of pastel

184

purple. The bletilla has now put on a star performance in my garden for over twenty years, during which it has thrived in several different sites, required division or thinning only once in ten years, and come undamaged through all that the region subjects it to in the way of bugs, diseases, moles, voles, rabbits, turtles, cats, dogs, and small neighborhood boys on mischief bent. Equally tolerant of weather described by an early settler as "excessive heat, excessive cold, and other irregularities in abundance," it needs, and fully earns, my help only in throwing a protective sheet over it at night when late spring frost threatens its tender, emerging shoots.

My other star purple-flowered performer, *Verbena* 'Violet Purple' ('Homestead' is similar), has been hardy through several winters, but only just. It makes a sheet of purple in late spring, then flowers intermittently through summer and autumn. Long trailing stems root as they go, which makes it easy to pot up a piece to winter indoors as a safeguard. I

Rich, not gaudy, is this combination of cream-and-purple ornamental cabbages, with an echo from the purple drumsticks of *Allium schoenoprasum* 'Forescate'. (Vail Alpine Garden, Colorado; August)

planted a big patch alongside a mulch path on the south-facing side of a large *Magnolia × soulangiana,* echoed by the pale purple flowers of *Erysimum* 'Bowles' Mauve'. This bushy, woody-based perennial or subshrub is not hardy in cold regions, nor long-lived anywhere, but it grows rapidly from cuttings and flowers month after month. Marking the corner of this bed is gray-leaved *Buddleia alternifolia* 'Argentea', usually a large shrub or small tree but here kept cut back as a two-foot shrub. In spite of the annual decapitation, it manages to produce some pale lavender flowers, creating a further echo with the verbena trailing around it. Mauve colchicums, which flower in September and October, grow up through the verbena, succeeding a mauve-flowered ornamental onion, *Allium stellatum*.

Erysimum 'Bowles' Mauve' echoes *Verbena* 'Violet Purple', the combination gaining zest from the chartreuse foliage of golden oregano (*Origanum vulgare* 'Aureum') edging the mulch path. (My garden; May)

Before the verbena was planted, *Cuphea hyssopifolia* was put out each year behind the golden oregano edging the bed and I wholeheartedly recommend it for frost-free regions or as a bedding plant. A neat little shrublet, with tiny bright green leaves and small purple flowers, it flowers without flagging, through heat and drought, from late spring into winter.

Other plants in the mauve to purple color range growing in the vicinity include *Liatris microphylla,* a dainty fine-leaved autumn-flowering species, about eighteen inches high when grown in sun and sand, and the trailing *Verbena tenuisecta* 'Edith'. Some years the bushy little aromatic lavender-flowered *Conradina verticillata* is a plant of which I can be proud. It gets gaunt after two or three years and needs replanting more deeply. Beyond the magnolia's canopy, where

Just around the bend from the picture opposite, *Verbena bonariensis* comes into bloom a bit later, along with poppies having pale mauve petals with a purple eye. (June)

Poppies, beaten down by heavy rain, lean picturesquely over the golden oregano. (June)

there's more "sky room," lavender-purple *Verbena bonariensis* keeps company with a pale mauve, purple-eyed poppy.

Verbena bonariensis has enjoyed the horticultural limelight for a good many years, and deservedly. Near it grows a newer introduction, *Lantana trifolia,* that "deserves to be better known," as gardening books so often say. In my experience plants of merit seldom remain obscure for long, the ripples spreading rapidly out as each recipient of something new in turn passes it on. This one was given to me by plantsman Tim Jennings and I've already passed it on to several friends. Technically it is a shrub, but for practical purposes it is an annual and must either be grown afresh from seed each year or carried over as cuttings. I root cuttings in October and keep them under lights indoors. In the course of a season it forms a bush some three to four feet high, liberally scattered from summer to frost with lavender flowers in spikes so congested they appear dome-shaped. The flowers develop into showy two- to three-inch banana-shaped clusters of violet fruits—the same showy and unusual color as callicarpa berries. Both are present on the bush, charming echoes of each other, from July until frost kills the plants.

As with other colors, bold or subtle echoes can also be

188

created by combining two plants of visually identical color but different form. In an English garden, in September, a colchicum with purple speckles and striations on a paler background grew up through the small but numerous purple flowers of an oregano (*Origanum laevigatum*) sprawling over the edge of a path. In my own garden *Penstemon hirsutus,* with flowers of pale lavender and cream held on upright stems, flowers at the same time as *Buddleia alternifolia* 'Argentea', which has arching branches strung with clusters of similarly colored small flowers. This is an easy penstemon but, in my garden anyway, it must be divided every year. I forgot to do this and am now rebuilding my stock from the sole survivor of my neglect.

Gardening involves a constant process of evaluation, measuring the cost in time and money against the reward. If one plant fails, immediately or, unaccountably, after several years of doing well, there are always other plants and combinations waiting to be tried. The interchangeability of the plants in the preceding "purple" pictures indicates how the selection process is simplified once a color theme is in place. Limiting the number of colors used still leaves abundant scope for artistry, while reducing the risk of mismatched colors.

In autumn colchicums rise up through the golden oregano. Colchicums, which are poisonous to humans, also seem to be avoided by voles, making them a better choice than autumn-flowering crocuses for vole-ridden gardens. (September)

189

The border in June. The border curves to a point in the foreground. At the point is a mound of evergreen *Ilex crenata* 'Helleri Gold' underplanted with golden thyme. Next to it is *Ruta graveolens* 'Curly Girl', echoed by the large blue-gray leaves of *Rudbeckia maxima.* The white at the far end is a self-sown *Lychnis coronaria* 'Alba' which I hadn't the heart to pull out.

The Unfolding of Two Echoes Borders  4

That beds and borders start with graph paper and a list of plants is more theory than fact. Professional designers, experienced in what grows well and combines well in their region, may do it that way, with everything planted in one fell swoop. You'll then have a planting known to work well—give or take idiosyncratic weather patterns—within ground rules laid down by the client, which frequently include minimal maintenance. If failure can't be risked, the planting will inevitably be stereotyped to some degree—beautiful, perhaps, but not uniquely yours unless you regard it as only the foundation on which you will build.

Many home gardeners begin by assembling a cheerful conglomeration of whatever they are given by friends or take a fancy to at local garden centers, sometimes continuing to be happy with this but often refining the collection gradually over the years.

The color conscious usually find it easiest to start with a small group of plants, gradually adding further plants and groupings within the chosen color scheme. For years I hovered over echo groupings in other gardens without analyzing what it was I liked about them, meantime assembling such groupings in my own garden more or less subconsciously. During the last few years two borders have come into being in intentional pursuance of the echoes theme. Here, in words and pictures, is the way they developed, starting with what inspired them and ending with recent or intended changes. In both borders there is considerable emphasis on foliage plants.

My inspiration. *Kniphofia* 'Little Maid', *Symphytum* × *uplandicum* 'Variegatum', and *Scabiosa ochroleuca*. A perfect example of echoing color, contrasting form. (Eleanor Carnwath, Seattle, Washington; July)

Cream and Yellows Border

Several years ago I lingered over a grouping in Eleanor Carnwath's Seattle garden, taking picture after picture. The key plant was a small torch lily, *Kniphofia* 'Little Maid', described this way by Beth Chatto, who introduced it: "The creamy flower spikes are very slender, flowering half-way down the total length of stem, which is barely two feet. It has fine grassy foliage, and is excellent for small gardens or small arrangements." Her words understated its charm and it went on to become one of the most popular of all torch lilies. Behind it Eleanor had placed a comfrey (*Symphytum* × *uplandicum* 'Variegatum') with bold green leaves broadly rimmed with cream. Alongside the torch lily was *Scabiosa ochroleuca*, its airy sprays of small creamy pompons a marked contrast in form with the slender spikes and bold leaves of its companions. *Solidaster* × *hybridus,* with masses of small yellow flowers that fade to cream, was also part of the grouping.

I wanted to copy this composition, but the creamy edges of the comfrey leaves scorch in southern heat, the torch lily, more fragile than most, has so far resisted my blandishments, and the solidaster fades too fast when weather gets hot. I hadn't then tried the scabious but it was apparent that this combination couldn't be replicated in my garden.

The creamy theme stayed at the back of my mind, and

192

the following spring I noticed how well the foliage of *Sedum alboroseum* 'Mediovariegatum' echoed the striped leaves of *Iris pallida* 'Variegata' (also sold as 'Aureavariegata', and sometimes as 'Zebra') which has stripes that look yellow when backlit but buttery when the sun comes from the front. The two were not then growing together. They were moved to form the nucleus of a new border. The sedum–iris combination has proved to be a good one for practical as well as color reasons. In my region the leaves of bearded irises tip-scorch and look shabby as summer progresses. By then the sedum has grown tall enough to draw attention away from them. A mishmash of variegated foliage gives a cluttered, confusing impression, with no one plant giving of its best, so variegated plants are often best displayed set against plainer ones, but the juxtapositioning of two variegated plants of similar color but markedly different shape or texture can work extremely well.

The place chosen for this border—perhaps forced upon me would be more accurate, it being the only fairly empty space awaiting occupants at the time—faces more or less east, with sun from the south also reaching it in the middle of the day. It is on a slight slope, backed by shrubs, well drained and sometimes dry toward the back, moist but never sodden along the front, where a path was made by digging out two feet of soil, tossing this up to form the bank, then filling the resulting ditch with sawdust topped with pine bark mulch. Oak-leaved hydrangeas (*Hydrangea quercifolia*) at the back are underplanted with daffodils, and under a deciduous holly with very thirsty roots, *Ilex verticillata* 'Red Sprite', is my perennial of last resort for dry shade, *Symphytum grandiflorum*. This will put up with places too dry and shady for most plants, opening its tubular cream flowers before shrubs and trees come into leaf. Yellow and pale orange, double and single Welsh poppies (*Meconopsis cambrica*) grow among the suckering stems of another background shrub, *Aronia arbutifolia*, which has red berries to strike a cheerful note through winter.

The starting echo. *Sedum alboroseum* 'Mediovariegatum' with *Iris pallida* 'Aureavariegata'. (May)

193

Above
An old bearded iris passed locally from garden to garden, name unknown, echoes the yellow eye of *Narcissus* 'Flower Record' growing under oak-leaved hydrangeas. (April)

Right
Rosa 'Graham Thomas' is echoed by a selected warm yellow form of *Portulaca oleracea*. (June)

Above
The early flowering *Hemerocallis dumortieri*. To its left is the foliage of *Scabiosa ochroleuca*. (May)

Left
Camassia leichtlinii 'Flore-pleno' adds its cream-flowered spikes to the picture. The grayish plant near the bottom of the picture is *Ballota pseudodictamnus*, a foliage plant that remains attractive all through the growing season. The fine foliage near the top is blue-flowered *Amsonia ciliata*. (June)

Above
Hosta 'Shade Fanfare' adds a further echo to the sedum and iris. Other plants include *Achillea* 'Great Expectations', *Ballota pseudodictamnus,* the bronzed foliage of *Crocosmia* 'Solfatare', *Liriope muscari* 'Variegata', *Dracocephalum rupestre, Pratia pedunculata, Gelsemium rankinii,* and *Sisyrinchium californicum.* (June)

Right
Liriope muscari 'Variegata' provides echoing color and contrasting form with *Hosta* 'Shade Fanfare', while *Dracocephalum rupestre* adds contrasting color. (June)

Mat-forming *Pratia pedunculata* echoes the deeper blue flowers of *Dracocephalum rupestre*. (June)

Rosa 'Graham Thomas' was already in place when the border was begun. This exquisite rose is of a yellow warm and rich but never gaudy, with apricot or amber tones at the heart, fading to somewhere between primrose and straw yellow. It flowers profusely in May and June and continues, less abundantly, until hard frost. Colors, I decided, would run toward warm but not brassy yellows, tans and browns in one direction, and creamy or lemon yellows in the other, supplemented with blue flowers and chartreuse foliage.

The rose was at first underplanted with *Santolina* 'Edward Bowles', which has gray-green foliage and pale primrose flowers. The colors were harmonious and the sizes and shapes well balanced, but fallen rose petals piled up on the santolina, causing the foliage to rot. For one season a selection of *Portulaca oleracea* that echoed the deeper tints in the rose was used as an underplanting. After growing different forms of the portulaca for a few years, self-sown seedlings now

July is peak daylily time in this region. These two are 'Mary Todd' and 'Golden Chimes', echoing *Heliopsis* 'Gold Feather', which has just come into bloom. (July)

appear each spring, with new colors appearing and old ones disappearing year by year. A sizable patch of preferred colors can be made within a few weeks simply by poking cuttings into the ground and watering them in. They need no further attention. This particular warm yellow didn't occur again and I'd failed to carry it over under lights through winter, as I usually do with my favorite colors. Golden lemon balm (*Melissa officinalis* 'Allgold') is the present underplanting. A vigorous foliage plant, it maintains its good appearance all through summer and autumn if cut back once when it gets straggly. After days of self-debate over daylilies in the nursery bed, I picked out one called 'Canyon Lands', gold and tan with a dark purple eye band, as companion for the lemon balm.

The border curves and comes to a point where another border goes off on a similar curve. A mound of chartreuse *Ilex crenata* 'Helleri Gold' was already in place on the point,

Above
Moving toward the cooler colors,
Hemerocallis 'Suzie Wong' is echoed by
Potentilla recta 'Sulphurea'. (June/July)

Left
Looking back from around the point,
Achillea 'Great Expectations' and
Hemerocallis 'Suzie Wong' are seen
through *Verbena bonariensis* (syn. *V.
patagonica*). (June/July)

Hemerocallis 'Milk Chocolate' is just coming into bloom. Its echo plant is *Carex buchananii,* just visible bottom left. The lower lily is 'Cream Tiger', the buds in the middle are 'Thunderbolt', and the tall one at the back is 'Anaconda'. (July)

underplanted with golden thyme. The thyme spreads rapidly but rots out in patches in summer and must be reset fairly often to keep it dense and in the right place. Other plants with golden green or creamy foliage include the low-growing, blue-flowered *Veronica* 'Trehane', *Liriope muscari* 'Variegata', blue-flowered *Iris tectorum* 'Variegatum', and, at

200

Hemerocallis 'Milk Chocolate' with *Hosta* 'Shade Fanfare' (July)

the front where the soil is moist, *Hosta* 'Shade Fanfare' and an iris called 'Ikai'. A hybrid between the Japanese iris (*Iris ensata*) and the yellow flag iris (*I. pseudacorus*), it marries the elegance of its Japanese parent with the sturdy constitution and adaptability of the yellow-flowered European. The three- to four-foot leaf blades are colored a delectable creamy chartreuse, reminding me of the heart of a homegrown buttercrunch lettuce. The flowers, of flat, Japanese iris form, are pale primrose with brown-fringed deeper yellow centers.

Cream and creamy or warm yellows, tans or browns include vase-shaped tawny *Carex buchananii*, *Achillea* 'Great Expectations', *Scabiosa ochroleuca* (which proved to be as happy in my garden as it is in Seattle), *Heliopsis* 'Gold Feather', bronze-leaved *Crocosmia* 'Solfatare', *Sisyrinchium californicum*, *Sedum* 'Weihenstephaner Gold', *Lilium* 'Cream Tiger', *Camassia leichtlinii* 'Flore Pleno', *Phlomis russeliana*, the chunky yellow blackberry lily *Belamcanda flabellata* and its

201

Right
The earlier daylilies have finished flowering but the tall, late *Hemerocallis altissima* 'Minaret' is now in bloom, joined by *Crocosmia* 'Solfatare', while *Heliopsis* 'Gold Feather' continues to bloom and *Achillea* 'Great Expectations' is on its second flowering after being cut back earlier. (August 1992)

Below
Flowering times can vary by as much as a month, occasionally more. The previous picture showed *Crocosmia* 'Solfatare' and *Hemerocallis* 'Minaret' blooming in August. The following year, after a very mild winter, they bloomed in July. The leaves of *Iris tectorum* 'Variegatum', bottom left, are cream and chartreuse in spring, becoming green by midsummer. (July 1993)

taller hybrids, the exquisite *Chrysanthemum rubellum* 'Mary Stoker' with hints of apricot in its creamy yellow flowers, and the evergreen jessamine, *Gelsemium rankinii,* which flowers in spring and a bit again in fall. This is a vine but by dint of cutting back the trailing strands it can be maintained as a mound. Daylilies in this color range include 'Mary Todd', the more graceful 'Golden Chimes' and 'Boutonniere', the unusual brown 'Milk Chocolate', a yellow-and-cinnamon bicolor of unknown name, the very early, compact, fragrant *Hemerocallis dumortieri,* and the tall and elegant, very late *H. altissima* 'Minaret'. The fine foliage of *Amsonia hubrectii* adds its quota of harvest gold in autumn.

Greenish or primrose yellows include *Hemerocallis* 'Suzie Wong', *Potentilla recta* 'Sulphurea', and one of the toughest, most trouble-free perennials I've ever grown, *Sedum aizoon.*

Blue flowers include *Centaurea montana, Amsonia ciliata, A. hubrectii, Dracocephalum rupestre,* violet-blue *Salvia* 'May Night', *Pratia pedunculata,* and *Echinops ruthenicus.* A prom-

I was just in time to catch the last flowers of *Digitalis ferruginea* keeping company with *Lilium* 'Thunderbolt' in Joanne Walkovic's garden. The lily has already taken its place in my border and the foxglove, grown from seed, will join it soon. (Pennsylvania; Late July)

ising new veronica from Soviet Georgia, *Veronica pedunculata* 'Georgia Blue' (also called 'Oxford Blue' in England), was recently added. It has small, shiny, dark green leaves on trailing, wiry stems that root as they go, forming a loose, low mound that kept its leaves and bore a few scattered flowers, small but brilliant gentian blue, through a mild winter, with its peak display in very early spring.

When, in a friend's garden, I saw the lily 'Thunderbolt' partnered with *Digitalis ferruginea,* I couldn't wait to add this combination. The lily went in that autumn, and while I was ordering lilies I also bought the taller 'Anaconda', with coppery apricot flowers. In Brian Bixley's Canadian garden I saw *Iris pallida* ('Aureavariegata') combined with creamy-belled *Onosma echioides* and I'm trying to find a space to fit the onosma in. The much vaunted *Hemerocallis* 'Stella de Oro', at present tucked into a temporary corner, may finally come to rest in this border. Truth to tell it is not a favorite of mine, nor, in my garden, is its performance all that is claimed, and I find it a difficult color to place. It would fit in here, though, and perhaps then I'll like it better.

Hot-Colors Border

My hot-colors border runs halfway across the front of the lot, with a post-and-rail fence behind. It measures 150 feet across, with roughly eighty feet of this occupied by shrubs at the two ends. It is fifteen feet deep in the middle, curving out to be wider at the ends. It faces due south. To its right is the drive, and on the other side of that, visually quite separate, is a border based on pink. To its left is a narrow path going through to a tree-lined shady walk which parallels the fenced west (east-facing) boundary.

It began with the evergreen goldthread cypress (*Chamaecyparis pisifera* 'Filifera Aurea') at one end and a group of three semievergreen *Abelia* 'Francis Mason' at the other.

Left
An early stage of the border, with *Chamaecyparis pisifera* 'Filifera Aurea', *Canna* 'Striata', the foliage of 'Redlette' daylilies, and a triangle of *Euonymus* 'Sparkle 'n' Gold' to echo the shape and color of the conifer. The need to screen out the road is apparent. (October)

Below
The daylilies have been interplanted with tulip 'Queen of Sheba' and the same tulips repeated in front of *Spiraea japonica* 'Gold Flame' at the other end. Columbines (*Aquilegia canadensis*) are also in bloom. (April)

Five years later the abelias (pruned a bit each winter) are four feet high. A red tip (*Photinia* × *fraseri* 'Red Robin') has since been planted in the middle of the abelias, going in as a young plant from a quart container. Potentially a very large shrub or small tree, it is hard pruned every year, so that it adds just a few branches of coppery new growth to contrast with the abelia's yellow leaves.

Canna 'Striata' ('Pretoria') went in next. It came as a gift from Henry Ross who, singlehandedly, has made and maintains Gardenview Horticultural Park in Strongsville, Ohio (open regularly to members and welcoming new ones, by appointment to others), where a great many choice plants can be seen. Against the goldthread cypress seemed the obvious place for the canna. The green and yellow striations of the canna leaves echo the stringlike chartreuse foliage of the cypress at the same time that their simple shape and bold size are in marked contrast. The canna is thinned out at the back each autumn to prevent it from crowding and rotting the cypress foliage. It then gets a six-inch mulch to help ensure its survival should winter be unusually cold. The canna has orange flowers, so the theme was now set: golden green would be the basic color, uniting the hot colors of red, orange, bright golden yellow, and, as modifiers, dark reddish brown or coppery purple.

Next to go in was the coppery red daylily *Hemerocallis* 'Redlette'. This draws attention to a pencil-fine edging of red on the canna leaves that otherwise would probably go unnoticed. The flowers of 'Redlette' shrivel neatly and daily deadheading is not needed.

Then a catalogue description of *Euonymus* 'Sparkle 'n' Gold' proved irresistible and a single plant was purchased. The gold-and-green foliage takes on orange tints in winter. Admiring this one winter day, I saw that I could make an echo in shape, reversing on the ground the pyramidal shape of the conifer, as if reflected in water. Euonymus cuttings root quickly and by planting them fairly thickly this was accomplished within a year. Later, when a paving edge was

Tulip 'Queen of Sheba' in front of *Spiraea japonica* 'Gold Flame', with single-flowered, yellow *Kerria japonica* in the background. (April)

put in, letting the euonymus grow right up to it would have spoiled its echo shape, but the gap needed filling. After musing on this for a while, black mondo grass (*Ophiopogon planiscapus* 'Nigrescens') emerged as the solution. Such dark recessive colors, used in contrast to brighter color, can disguise or alter perceived contours. It is also a flattering contrast to the occasional wandering bright gold strand of the euonymus.

It bothered me to see the road outside the fence. Two groups of evergreen, red-berried nandinas screen it out in part but could not be placed where they would hide the vines on the fence. These include scarlet and yellow trumpet honeysuckles (*Lonicera sempervirens* 'Magnifica', *L.s.* 'John Clayton',

As seen from outside the fence, with *Kerria japonica* 'Pleniflora' in the narrow border running at right angles. (April)

and the hybrid 'Dropmore Scarlet'), and the evergreen, yellow-flowered Carolina jessamine (*Gelsemium sempervirens*). Outside the fence there's a shallow bank about eighteen inches wide, sloping down into a drainage ditch which is often full of water. This offered scant foothold for a shrub. The problem was solved with *Miscanthus sinensis* 'Zebrinus'. The chartreuse bands in its leaf blades provide another color echo, and it doesn't mind having part of its roots submerged in water from time to time, in fact it prefers this to dry soil.

Mine is a grassless garden and my unwillingness to mow extends to the roadside verge, so the grass was killed with Roundup and the verge planted with Japanese weeping love grass (*Eragrostis curvula*), interplanted with the tough, rapidly spreading tawny daylilies, *Hemerocallis fulva* 'Europa', and

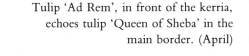

Tulip 'Ad Rem', in front of the kerria, echoes tulip 'Queen of Sheba' in the main border. (April)

Left
Narcissus 'Ambergate' is tucked in close to the kerria. (April)

Below
In a shaded part of the extended border *Narcissus* 'Jet Fire' continues the hot-color theme, with its flung-back yellow petals echoed by the evergreen fans of *Acorus gramineus* 'Ogon'. (April)

Right
Hemerocallis 'Redlette' is in bloom, drawing attention to a pencil-fine red margin on the canna leaf which otherwise would pass unnoticed. (June)

Below
Hemerocallis 'Screech Owl' comes hot on the heels of 'Redlette', the yellow petal edges echoing the yellow in the canna leaves. Self-sowing *Coreopsis lanceolata* is in bloom in the background. (June)

double-flowered 'Kwanso Florepleno' to continue the hot color theme of the border inside the fence. After three years the daylilies have crowded out most weeds and almost crowded out the weeping love grass. This was supposed to be a self-sufficient planting and it almost is, but after the daylilies have finished flowering their forest of dead stems look so unsightly that I feel compelled to remove them. The ditch itself was stuffed with blue, yellow, and coppery red moisture-loving irises: *Iris versicolor, I. pseudacorus,* and various Louisiana irises including *I. fulva.*

At the other end of the border from the goldthread cypress, *Spiraea* 'Gold Flame' was planted in front of the yellow abelias, and the single-flowered *Kerria japonica* put tight against the fence behind. This kerria, unlike the double-flowered *K.j.* 'Pleniflora', flowers only once, in early spring, but in summer it seems to bear masses of small scarlet tubular flowers from a vigorous but dainty vine, *Manettia cordifolia,* that twines among the kerria branches.

The columbines in the foreground briefly echoed the scarlet honeysuckle on the fence (*Lonicera sempervirens* 'Magnifica'). Now they are over and *Achillea* 'Coronation Gold' provides contrast. (May/June)

To echo the coppery new growth of the spiraea, I planted the lily-flowered tulip 'Queen of Sheba', interplanting the bulbs with *Aquilegia canadensis*. The foliage of this scarlet-and-yellow columbine stays fresh all season long and it hides the withering leaves of the tulips. The tulips diminish in number most years (during a very wet season they actually increased), so they are "topped up" with a few more each autumn.

The same tulips were added at the other end, interplanting them with the 'Redlette' daylilies, with a few outriders tucked among the euonymus. Daylilies are the best perennial I know for interplanting with tulips or daffodils. They don't need dividing very often and the foliage grows up at just the right time to hide the dying leaves of the bulbs. With daffodils the disguise is aided by the similarity in shape of daffodil and daylily leaves.

Borders are often viewable from more than one angle. There are more columbines at the conifer end of the border and from one angle of view the tulips are seen against a background of these and, on the fence behind, the scarlet honeysuckle. By the time the columbines have finished flowering, *Achillea* 'Coronation Gold' has come into bloom, contrasting with the honeysuckle. The wisdom of experience dictates that the seed heads now be removed from the columbines, to obviate the need for hours spent removing unwanted seedlings. For one year the achillea was interplanted with orange lilies. Rodents ate them. There's no status quo in gardening. Choice lilies are now planted in sunken containers. Inexpensive ones take their chance.

In April, with taller perennials still dormant and the honeysuckles on the fence not yet fully leafed out, parts of the border are open to view from outside the fence. From this angle the tulips are seen against the double-flowered *Kerria japonica* 'Pleniflora' across the path from the goldthread cypress.

Spiraea 'Golden Princess' was planted center front of the border but this has since been removed. It is a first-rate shrub, healthy and trouble-free with attractive golden green foliage. When it grew out of proportion I might have kept it pruned had there not been other counts against it: its flowers are pink—a paler pink than *S.* 'Gold Flame' but still wrong for this border. Also, being deciduous, it left a gap in the punctuating yellow foliage along the front of the border. It was replaced with a group of three yellow-striped yuccas, *Yucca* 'Bright Edge', interplanted with orange-flowered crocuses. The magenta flowers of *Spiraea* 'Gold Flame' are now the only pink in this border, endured because the coppery new growth is a highlight of the year.

June and July are the main daylily months. *Hemerocallis* 'Screech Owl' is very showy against the backlit leaves of the canna. 'Pappy Gates' made a charmingly subtle echo with the fading flowers of the achillea and with the golden yellow daisies of a heliopsis. It has, nonetheless, now been removed,

At the end of the border, where there is afternoon shade, the goldthread cypress is underplanted with golden creeping charlie (*Lysimachia nummularia* 'Aurea'). This is interplanted with the dark-leaved *Ranunculus ficaria* 'Brazen Hussy' for early spring display, and with the dusky-flowered *Viola* 'Molly Sanderson' for late spring and summer. (September)

being one of the large number of daylilies (the majority, in fact) that offends with the "wet socks" effect of the spent flowers, a description from Elisabeth Sheldon in her book *A Proper Garden* that sums it up exactly. This characteristic, always a flaw, becomes completely unacceptable to me in daylilies set back in a border, where one must daily risk trampling other plants to keep them presentable.

Other summer flowers in the border include the red daylily 'Palace Guard', red *Achillea* 'The Beacon', yellow *Rudbeckia fulgida* 'Newmanii' (similar to 'Goldsturm' but staying more neatly in its clump), *Curtonus paniculatus* (similar to *Crocosmia* 'Lucifer' but taller), *Gaillardia* 'Burgundy', *Coreopsis lanceolata,* the orange blackberry lily (*Belamcanda chinensis*), *Potentilla* 'Gibson's Scarlet', the feathery-leaved scarlet-flowered spires of the biennial standing cypress, *Ipomopsis rubra,* an orange torch lily (*Kniphofia*), butterfly weed (*Asclepias tuberosa*), and coppery red *Helenium* 'Dunkelpracht'. Red and orange dahlias flower all summer but are at their best in autumn, joined by chrysanthemums and *Coreopsis integrifolia.* When frost blackens their leaves, the dahlia tubers are lifted, put into buckets, covered with sand or bark fines, and stored in the laundry room through winter.

A recent addition, filling the gap alongside the path where the conifer casts shade for much of the day, is the golden creeping charlie, *Lysimachia nummularia* 'Aurea'. In sunnier parts of the garden this had scorched in summer. An interplanting of the almost black *Viola* 'Molly Sanderson'— a suggestion of Allen Lacy's in his *The Garden in Autumn*— has been a great success; its dark petals stand out against the gold of the creeping charlie, with an echo from the yellow eye. The viola isn't long-lived but it is easily propagated by cuttings.

As ripples spread out from a stone thrown into a pond, so does one idea flow from another, and the success of this combination prompted me to add more near black, this time from the leaves of *Ranunculus ficaria* 'Brazen Hussy'. The dark purple rosettes of this form of the English celandine appear

in January, followed in March and April by varnished golden starry flowers. By the end of May it has gone neatly to rest until the following year. I mean to try growing this and the viola through golden Scotch moss (*Arenaria verna* 'Aurea'), if and when I get around to it. A dainty lily (*Lilium pumilum*), with scarlet turks-cap flowers on slender eighteen-inch stems also pierces through the creeping charlie, flowering in June.

Gardeners seldom rest content and there always seem to be more plants-in-waiting than places available for them, so before long the chartreuse-based hot-color theme was extended down the narrow, east-facing, shrub-backed border running at right angles to the existing border. *Kerria japonica* 'Pleniflora' marks the sunny end, then it becomes progressively shadier, becoming sunny again where it meets up with the cream-based border previously described. The shady section is a suitable place for such hostas as 'Frances Williams', echoed by the yellow blades of *Carex elata*

The near black flowers of *Viola* 'Molly Sanderson' stand out against the creeping charlie, while the yellow eye provides a minor echo. (May, continuing through summer)

215

Right
Hemerocallis 'Pappy Gates' blooms in mid- to late summer. Here it echoes *Helianthus* 'Gold Feather' in the center of the border. (July/August)

'Aurea' (*Carex stricta* 'Bowles' Golden'), and *Hosta montana* 'Aureomarginata'. It is punctuated by clumps of the evergreen *Acorus gramineus* 'Ogon'.

A P.S. to the description of my hot-color border. Words that I've heard so many times are "Oh, but that's not hardy for us." *Canna* 'Striata', a keynote plant in my border, is at its best in the warm, moist Southeast, and it isn't hardy much beyond zone 8, but although it must be lifted and stored in cold regions, and does not attain the same size where summers are dry or the growing season short, this does not preclude its use, it is just used differently, as one of the pictures shows.

Such borders are not static, never quite the same, in fact, for two years in a row. One plant may be substituted for another for many different reasons. Replacements must be found for those that don't do well or look as well as one hoped, or those which have performed well in the past but have inexplicably gone into decline. Irresistible new plants come along and a place is found for them, or one becomes newly aware of the possibilities in a plant owned for years but never used effectively. The seasonal balance may need changing, or a color theme may have become too bland, calling for more contrast. And always the search goes on for plants that give a good account of themselves—more often

Above
The last daylily to bloom is
Hemerocallis altissima 'Minaret', shown
here with *Kerria japonica* 'Pleniflora',
which, unlike other kerrias which
flower only in spring, continues to
bear a smattering of bloom through
summer and autumn. (August)

Left
Dahlia 'Bishop of Llandaff' starts
blooming in midsummer but is at its
best when the days cool in autumn. In
August and September it is joined by
Helenium 'Dunkle Pracht'. There is still
a scattering of flowers on the trumpet
honeysuckle, and the self-sowing
biennial *Rudbeckia triloba* has just come
into bloom. (August)

217

This single-flowered orange Korean chrysanthemum is color-matched to the small soft orange tubular flowers of *Dicliptera suberecta,* with *Dahlia* 'Bishop of Llandaff' providing a note of brighter color. None of these is reliably hardy. The dahlia tubers are lifted and wintered indoors, and cuttings of the other two are rooted in autumn and wintered under lights. They grow fast when put out in spring. (November)

with foliage than with flowers, for the longest possible time, with the minimum of spraying or other repetitive maintenance.

My cream and yellows border is still being refined. The middle part of the hot-color border is being reworked, in part in the constant search for those plants that give the most and ask the least, but mostly because my garden is also my studio and experimental station and there are so many plants waiting to be tried, combined, and photographed. The "bones," however, remain in the evergreen punctuating plants, consisting of the goldthread cypress at one end, the golden abelias at the other, and, spaced in between, the 'Sparkle 'n' Gold' euonymus, *Yucca* 'Bright Edge' (group of three), and three little blobs of the oh-so-slow *Ilex crenata* 'Golden Gem' which will, when size suffices, be reduced to one. The yellow form of *I.c.* 'Helleri' would have grown faster but the color is a less bright gold.

Garden compositions must reach some degree of maturity to be satisfying, but it is the changes, the new plants, the new ways of presenting them, that satisfy creative needs and make gardening such an absorbing, satisfying hobby. Discussions with friends and visits to other gardens bring fresh insights and inspiration, and seldom do I arrive home without a new plant or two. A plant or combination admired in another garden starts the mind churning, mulling over how best to incorporate it into one's own garden. Or the more complicated revamping process that goes "almost perfect, but . . . now if . . . ?"

And all the time one is learning to do it better. Only the ending of life itself writes "finished" to the story of a garden.

Autumn. There has been no frost yet. Nandinas at the back bear heavy trusses of scarlet berries. Other plants include *Coreopsis integrifolia*, annual yellow cosmos, *Dicliptera suberecta*, dahlias, *Chrysanthemum* 'Bronze Elegance', *Yucca* 'Bright Edge', *Spiraea* 'Golden Princess', and, outside the fence, *Miscanthus sinensis* 'Zebrinus'. (November)

Right
View from outside the fence, with *Canna* 'Striata' still in bloom, as it has been all summer, and *Miscanthus sinensis* 'Zebrinus' screening out the road (October)

Below
In a colder climate than mine, a pair of cannas in containers are color-matched to the golden robinias (*Robinia pseudoacacia* 'Frisia') flanking the steps to a patio. The cannas are underplanted with the trailing *Helichrysum petiolare* 'Limelight', which has gray leaves suffused with chartreuse, making a pale echo with the canna leaves. (Ellen McFarland, Massachusetts; September)

Index

Note: Page numbers in *italics* indicate illustrations.

Abelia 'Francis Mason', 204, 206, 211, 218
Abelmoschus 'Manihot Lemon Bowl', 71
Abutilon pictum 'Thompsonii', *93*
Abyssinian banana, *109*
Acanthopanax sieboldianus 'Variegatus', 74–76
Acer: japonicum 'Aureum', *153; negundo* 'Flamingo', 78; *palmatum*, 43, 78; *shirasawanum* 'Aureum', *153*
Achillea, 63, *80*, 88, *164*
Achillea: 'Anthea', 155; 'The Beacon', *92*, 165; 'Coronation Gold', *90*, 155, *155*, 183, *211*, 212; 'Creamy', *160*, 161; 'Gold Plate', *90*, 155; 'Great Expectations' ('Hoffnung'), 115, *196*, *199*, *202;* x *kellereri*, *13; millefolium*, 94; 'Moonshine', *13*, 155; 'Paprika', *165;* 'Salmon Beauty', *62*, 170
Aconitum, 174
Acorus gramineus, 67, 72, 148, *209*, 216
Actinidia kolomikta, 79, 81
Adiantum capillus-veneris, *103*

Agapanthus, 132
Agastache: 'Apricot Sunrise', *85*, 170; *coccinea, 164;* 'Firebird', 170
Ageratum, 132
Ajuga, 49, 112
Ajuga: 'Metallica Crispa Purpurea', 107; 'Minicrisp Purple', 107; 'Pink Elf', *95;* 'Pink Silver', 76; *reptans* 'Burgundy Glow', 76, *76*, 78; 'Rubra Contorta', 107
Alcea rugosa nigra, 114
Alchemilla, 106, *145*
Alchemilla mollis, 64, 80, 141, 150, *152*
Allium: multibulbosum (nigrum), 44, *45; schoenoprasum*, *11*, 112, *175, 185; sphaerocephalon*, 63, 109; *stellatum*, 186; *thunbergii*, 46–47
Alstroemerias, 99
Althaea ficifolia (rugosa), 40, 158
Amaranthus, *172*
Amaranthus caudatus, 76
Ambrosia, 105
Amsonia: ciliata, 195; hubrectii, 135, 203; *montana*, 158, 161; *orientalis*, 135; *tabernaemontana*, 135, *135*

Anaphalis, *122*
Anchusa, *53*
Angle of view, 12–13, 112, 212
Anthemis: 'Creamy', 158; 'Grallach Gold', *156;* 'Rebecca Broyles', *159, 160*, 161, *161; tinctoria* 'Wargrave', 155
Anthriscus sylvestris, 6
Aquilegia: caerulea, 139; *canadensis*, *14*, 74, *168, 205*, 212; *chrysantha*, 87; 'Double Burgundy', *110*, 112; *formosa*, *155; vulgaris*, 145
Arabis procurrens, 36, *95*
Arachniodes simplicior (aristata 'Variegata'*)*, 148
Aralia, five-leaved, 75
Aralia elata 'Aurea Variegata', *156*
Aronia arbutifolia, 193
Artemisia: abrotanum, 105; *canescens*, 121; 'Huntington', *99; indica* 'Variegata', 161; 'Powis Castle', *45*, 58, *118, 159; stelleriana, 119*, 177; 'Valerie Finnis', *53*
Arum italicum 'Pictum', 162, *163*, 164

Arundinaria (Pleioblastus) viridistriata, 93, 148

Arundo donax 'Variegata', 71

Asarum canadense, 104

Aster, 158, 161, 174

Aster: 'Alma Potschke', 90; *carolinianus*, 160; 'Hella Lacy', 95; *laevis*, 171; *oblongifolius* 'Raydon's Favorite', 171; 'Professor Kippenburg', 137, *159;* 'Purple Dome', 95

Astermoea mongolica (Kalimeris), 123

Astilbe, 62, *87, 122;* 'Cattleya', 177; 'Red Sentinel', 83

Astrantia, 123

Astrantia major, 72

Athyrium niponicum 'Pictum', *95,* 105

Aucuba, 82–83

Aucuba japonica 'Fructualbo', 82, *82*

Aurinia saxatilis, 87, 144

Autumn, 45–47

Azalea, 83, *86, 125;* 'Balsaminaeflora', 180; 'Ben Morrison', 48; evergreen, 32, 48, 177, 183, 184–185; 'Girard's Hot Shot', 32; 'Hampton Beauty', 180; 'Irene Koster', *172;* 'Koromo Shikibu', *39,* 184–185; 'Misty Plum', 183; orange, *145;* 'Rose Glow', 177

Ballota pseudodictamnus, 115–116, *195, 196*

Baptisia: australis, 133, *133; minor, 30,* 133

Barberry, 43; pink, 78–79; purple, 62, *64, 84, 84,* 105, 108, 112; yellow, 35–36, *86,* 141

Basil, purple, 36, 106–107

Basket-of-gold, *144*

Bearded iris, *50, 61, 101, 155,* 193, *194*

Bee balm, 177

Bee guides, 35, 39–40, *40*

Bells-of-Ireland, 105

Berberis: x *gladwynensis* 'William Penn', 43; 'Harlequin', 78; 'Pink Queen', 78; *thunbergii*, 35–36, 78–79, 84, *84, 86,* 105, *105,* 108, 141

Betula pendula 'Purpurea', 53

Birch, 53, *124,* 132

Black mondo grass, 108, *118,* 207

Blender colors, 16, 67, 97–101

Bletilla striata, 28, 54, *55,* 184–185

Blooming times, 29–30

Bluebells, 131

Bluebonnets, *131,* 132

Blue cedar, *118*

Blue flax, 136

Blue gardens, 130–140

Blue rue, 121

Boltonia: latisquama 'Nana', 171; 'Snowbank', *122, 159*

Borders: cream and yellows, 192–204, 218; design of, 191–192; hot-color, *14, 21, 164,* 204–218; mixed, *30, 80, 84, 98, 99*

Bowles' golden grass, *145,* 148, *153*

Bowles' golden sedge, 148

Bowman's root, 123

Boxwood, 85, *96*

Brightness, use of term, 22

Brown flowers, 115, 201

Brunnera macrophylla, 68, 135

Buddleia, *122*

Buddleia alternifolia 'Argentea', 186, 189

Burford holly, 43

Burnet, 114

Butterbur, *103*

Butterfly weed, 140, 168

Cabbage: ornamental, 60, *185;* purple, 106–107

Calamagrostis: acutiflora 'Karl Foerster', *51;* 'Overdam', 124

Calamintha: nepeta, 37–38, *134,* 158, *159; sylvatica*, 38

Callicarpa, 46–47

Callicarpa dichotoma, 46

Calliopsis, 61

Calylophus serrulatus, 88

Camassia leichtlinii 'Flore-pleno', *195*

Camellias, 83

Campanula: carpatica, 122; glomerata, 90; isophylla, 132; *lactiflora, 156; latifolia* 'Alba', *72; latiloba* 'Hidcote Amethyst', *182; persicifolia, 122; poscharskyana*, 28

Candytuft, *182*

Canna, 36, 107, 112, 158, *159, 160,* 161, *161, 210, 220*

Canna: flagellifera, 115; *glauca, 99;* 'Pfitzer Chinese Coral', 170; 'Striata' ('Pretoria'), *56,* 58, *205,* 206, 216, *220*

Cardinal flower, 133, 162

Carex: buchananii, 115, *169, 200; conica* 'Marginata', 68; *elata, 67,* 148, 215–216; *flagellifera,* 170; 'Frosted Curls', 76; *glauca,* 121; *siderosticta* 'Variegata', 70; 'Sparkler', *95; stricta* 'Bowles' Golden', 216

Carolina jessamine, 208

Caryopteris x *clandonensis, 7,* 137, 161

Cassia marilandica, 157

Catchflies, 54, 57, 180

Ceanothus, 132

Cedrus atlantica 'Glauca', *118*

Celandine, 90, *91,* 106, *213,* 214–215

Centranthus ruber, 72, 123

Cerastium tomentosum, 121, *122*

Ceratostigma: plumbaginoides, 135; *willmottianum,* 43, 135, 160

Chaenomeles 'Jet Trail', 70–71

Chamaecyparis: obtusa 'Crippsii', 102, 143; *pisifera* 'Filifera Aurea', *96,* 143, 204, *205*

Chartreuse, 100, 116–117, 140–154, 165

Chenopodium botrys, 105

Chinese elm, 46

Chionanthus, 45; *retusus serrulatus*, 127

Chives, *11, 175*

Choisya ternata, 66

Chrysanthemum, 37, 70, 158, *218*

Chrysanthemum: 'Apricot', 170; 'Bronze Elegance', 170, 174, *219; carinatum,* 61; *leucanthemum* 'May Queen', *54;* 'Mei Kyo', *179; pacificum,* 150; *parthenium* 'Aureum', *34,* 117, 145, 150; *rubellum* 'Mary Stoker', 203

Cirsium rivulare: atropurpureum, 114; *atrosanguineum*, 113

Clematis, 79, 184

Clematis: 'Betty Corning', 139; x *durandii,* 139; 'Etoile Violette', 139; 'Hagley Hybrid', 37; 'Mme. Julia Correvon', *179;* 'Perl d'Azur', 139; 'Purpurea Plena Elegans', 114; 'Ramona', 139; 'Royal Velours', 114

Cleome, 122

Cleome: 'Helen Campbell', *128;* 'Violet Queen', *176*

Climbing aster, 160

Climbing nasturtium, 146

Cohesion, 84–90, 123; foliage for, 6, 44, 115; and space, 95

Colchicums, 186, 189, *189*

Color, colors: basic, 99–100; fashions of, 4–8; as illusion, 17; mixed compositions of, 9–10, *80*, 81; theory of, 15–28; use of term, 22

Color wheel/chart, 16–33

Columbines, 74, 87, *110*, 112, *138*, 139, 144, *153, 168, 205, 211*, 212

Comfrey, 40–41, 192, *192*

Commelina tuberosa, 135

Complementary colors: defined, 24; orange and blue, 158, 160, 167–171; purple and yellow, 181, 183–187; red and green, *9*, 162

Coneflower, *122, 177*

Conifers, 85, 102, 141, *142*, 143

Conradina verticillata, 187

Continuity, 84–88, 115, *176*

Contrasts: colors, 23–24, *93*, 100, 146, *152, 196*; foliage for, 104; form, *12*, 90, *92*, 101, *133, 134, 156, 192, 193*; need for, 90–101; size, *34*, 112, *133*; and space, *92*, 94; texture, 90, *93, 95*, 101, 112, *116, 156*

Convolvulus mauritanicus, 132

Coordination, guidelines for, 16–17

Coralbells, *30, 50*

Coreopsis: 'Early Sunrise', *90; integrifolia, 219; lanceolata, 210;* 'Moonbeam', 106, 155, *158; tinctoria, 61; verticillata, 90*

Cornus: alba, 43, 44; florida, 31, 78, 166; *stolonifera*, 43, 44, *173*

Corydalis, *158*

Corylus maxima 'Purpurea', 112

Cosmos, *172, 219*

Cosmos: astrosanguineus, 114; *sulphureus, 90*

Cotinus coggygria, 62, *101*, 108; 'Grace', 160

Cotoneaster, *113*

Cow parsley, 6

Crambe cordifolia, 123

Creamy foliage, 70–76, 83, *89*, 99–100, 127, *130*

Creeping charlie, 73, *74*, 91, 141, *144, 148, 213*, 214, *215*

Crepe myrtle, *46*

Crimson gardens, 171–181

Crocosmia: 'Lucifer', 22, 162, *164;* 'Solfatare', *196, 202*

Crocus, 43, 189

Crocus chrysanthus, 43

Cupflower, *157*

Cuphea hyssopifolia, 187

Cupressus sempervirens 'Swane's Gold', *85*

Cytisus x *praecox* 'Warminster', 74

Daffodils, *154, 169*, 193, 212

Dahlia, 114, *122, 219*

Dahlia, 'Bishop of Llandaff', 106, 162, *217, 218*

Daisies: gloriosa, *34*; white, *54, 75*; yellow, *12, 109*, 213

Daphne: x *burkwoodii* 'Carol Mackie', *95; caucasica, 147; odora, 173*

Daucus carota, 168

Daylily, *12, 51, 61*, 62, *62*, 88, 114, 158, 161, 168, 170, *198; see also Hemerocallis*

Delphinium, 132

Delphinium grandiflorum, 167

Dentaria diphylla, 129, *129*

Deutzia gracilis, 70, 127

Dianthus, *53, 164*

Dianthus: barbatus, 33, 114, 171; 'Bat's Double Red', *178; chinensis*, 115; *deltoides, 158;* 'Inchmery', *121;* 'King of the Blacks', 165, *165*

Diascia vigilis, 13

Dicentra spectabilis 'Alba', *125*, 164

Dicliptera suberecta, 218, 219

Dictamnus, 30

Digitalis: ferruginea, 203, 204; *purpurea* 'Alba', 124

Dogwood, 43–45, *94, 96*, 129, *129*, 166

Dracaena, *116*

Dracocephalum rupestre, 136, *196, 197*

Dutch iris, 160, 161

Dwarf bamboo, *93*

Dwarf daffodil, *169*

Dwarf hebe, *119*

Dwarf purple osier, *110*

Dwarf yaupon, 85

Dyssodia tenuiloba, 109

Eccremocarpus scaber, 146

Echinacea purpurea, 122, 160–161, *161*, 177

Echinops, 134; *ritro*, 177

Echium vulgare, 132, 158

Echoes, defined, 2–3

Elaeagnus: angustifolia, 128; x *ebbingei* 'Gilt Edge', 43; *pungens* 'Maculata', *153*

Eleutherococcus, 74–76

Elijah's tears, 112

Elymus arenarius, 101

English bluebells, 131

English primrose, 77–78

English roses, 170

Ensete ventricosum 'Maurelii', *109*

Epilobium dodonaei, 101

Eragrostis curvula, 208

Eremurus stenophyllus, 101

Eriophyllum lanatum, 12

Eryngium giganteum, 64

Erysimum: 'Bowles' Mauve', *89*, 186, *186; helveticum*, 57, *57*, 87

Erytrichium: aretoides, 130; *nanum*, 130

Eucomis bicolor, 105

Euonymus, 21, 49, 62, 99, *153*

Euonymus: alatus, 47; *fortunei*, 49, 70–71, *128; japonicus* 'Microphyllus', 85; 'Sparkle 'n' Gold', *14, 205*, 206–207, 218

Eupatorium coelestinum, 132

Euphorbia, 58, 141, 149

Euphorbia: amygdaloides 'Rubra', 105; *characias, 153; dulcis* 'Chameleon', 106, 112; *epithymoides*, 151; *griffithii* 'Fireglow', 166; x *martinii*, 84; *myrsinites*, 143; *sequierana niciciana, 151; sikkimensis*, 42

European ginger, 104

European silver birch, 53

Evergreens, 49, 85, 141, *142*, 149, 183, *190*, 204, 218

Eyes: contrasts, 36, 198; echoes, *34*, 35, *56*, 58, *63, 187, 215*

Felicia amelloides, 132

Fennel, purple, 106–107, 112

Ferns, *69, 95, 103*, 104, *104*, 148, *163*, 164

Festuca, 121, *137*

Feverfew, *34*, 117, 145, 150

Firecracker vine, 146

Foliage: chartreuse, 116–117, 165; for cohesion, 6, 44, 97–101, 115; for contrast, 104; creamy echoes in, 70–76, 83, *89*, 99–100; gray echoes in, 115–121; pink echoes in, 76–79, 81, 83; purple echoes in, *52*, 105–114; red echoes in, *50, 210*; variegated, 67–81, *68*; veins in, 42, *56*, 58, 161; white echoes in, 23, *31*, 68–73, *69*, 124; yellow echoes in, *34*, *56*, 62, 91, *210*

Forget-me-nots, 130, 132, 166–167

Forsythia, *147, 154*

Foxglove, 35, 54, *55*, 61, 124, 127, *130, 203*

Fragaria, 'Pink Panda', 180

Fringe tree, 45

Fruits, echoes in, 42–43, 44, 46–47, *46, 82–83, 152*, 164

Fumaria officinalis, 181

Gaillardia: 'Burgundy', 36, *92, 164*, 165, *176*; 'Goblin', 36; 'Red Plume', *93*; 'Yellow Plume', *93*

Galium odoratum, 69, 70, *96*, 104

Gardens: color-coordinated, 11–12, *11, 12*; criticisms of, 4–5; functions, 3–4; natural, 4, 6–8

Gardner's garters, 44

Gaura lindheimeri, 37, 123

Gelsemium: rankinii, 196, 203; semper-virens, 208

Gentian, 130

Geranium, *49*

Geranium: clarkei 'Kashmir White', 123; *endressii, 30, 113; macrorrhizum* 'Ingwersen's Variety', *172*; x *mag-nificum, 138*; 'Mavis Simpson', *98*; *phaeum*, 114; *psilostemon, 177, 181*; *sanguineum, 175*, 177; *sessiliflorum* 'Nigricans', 107

Germander, *96*

Geum: x 'Borisii', 166, 167; 'Red Wings', *168*

Gillenia trifoliata, 123

Ginger: European, 104; wild, 104

Glaucium corniculatum, 164

Gleditsia triacanthos 'Sunburst', *86, 141, 144*

Globe amaranth, 42, 60

Globe thistle, *134, 177*

Gloriosa rothschildiana, 146–147

Glyceria aquatica 'Variegata', *130*

Golden bamboo, *148*

Golden gardens, 140–154, *142, 144, 145, 147*, 165

Golden honey locust, *86*, 141, *144*

Golden hop, *151*

Golden lemon balm, *169*, 198

Golden oregano, 100, *117*, 143, 144, *186, 188, 189*

Golden privet, *144*

Goldenrod, *12*

Golden thyme, 36, *143, 190*, 200

Goldthread cypress, 143, 144, 146, 204, 206, *213*, 218

Gomphrena globosa, 42, 60

Grass: in borders, *23*, 86–87; as echo, *51, 92, 118*, 121, *130, 174*; in golden gardens, 148–149, *157, 169*; purple, 108; in white gardens, 124

Gray echoes, 115–121

Green echoes, 63, 101–105

Hakonechloa macra 'Aureola', *99*, 148, 150, *151*

Harmony, 10, 16, 22–23, 25–26, 91, 100

Harsh color, toning down, *80*, 81

Hedera helix, 49, 69, *69*, 145–146, 184

Helenium: 'Dunkle Pracht', *217*; 'Ku-gelsonne' ('Sun Sphere'), 158; 'Moerheim Beauty', *64*

Helianthemum, 77

Helianthus 'Capenoch Star', 155, 158, *161*

Helichrysum petiolare 'Limelight', 120, *220*

Helictotrichon sempervirens, 118, 176

Heliopsis, *90*, 155, *198, 202*, 213

Heliotropium arborescens, 177

Hellebore, *163*, 164

Helleborus orientalis, 104, *173*

Hemerocallis: 'Aabachee', 63; *altissima* 'Minaret', *202*, 203, *217*; 'Amersham', *64*; 'Bonanza', *63*; 'Bouton-niere', 203; 'Canyon Lands', 198; 'Cape Cod', 114; 'Corky', 40, *64*, 155; *dumortieri, 195*, 203; 'Eric the Red', *64*, 110–111; *fulva, 51*, 208, 211; 'Golden Chimes', 155, *198*, 203; 'Icecap', 161; 'Joan Senior', 124; 'Little Grapette', 63; 'Loving Memories', *126*; 'Mary Todd', *198*, 203; 'Milk Chocolate', 115, *200, 201*, 203; 'Mme. Bellum', 40, *40*; 'Nashville', *64*, 110–111; 'Palace Guard', 165, 214; 'Pappy Gates', 213–214; 'Redlette', 205, 206, *210*, 212; 'Screech Owl', *210*, 213; 'Stafford', *64*, 110–111; 'Stella de Oro', *90*, 204; 'Suzie Wong', *199*, 203; 'Tetrina's Daughter', *156*

Hen-and-chickens, *52*

Heuchera, 30, 50; x *brizoides*, 177; 'Montrose Ruby', 106; 'Palace Purple', 49, *105, 109, 164*; 'Pluie de Feu', *90*; 'Shere Variety', 180; 'Un-improved', 177; *villosa*, 105

Hibiscus trionum, 36

Hieracium lanatum, 121

Hinoki cypress, 102, 143

Holly, 43, 47, 62, 99, *153*, 193

Hollyhock, 40, 114, 158

Honeysuckle, *145, 148*, 149, 177, 180, 207, *211, 212, 217*

Horehound, 183

Hosta, 18, *69*, 70, 72, 95, 102, *103*, 104, 121, *125*, 141, 143, 147–148, *153*, 166–167

Hosta: 'August Moon', 120, 184; *fluc-tuans* 'Variegata', 72; *fortunei* 'Aurea', 140; 'Francee', 73, *73*; 'Frances Williams', 215; 'Golden Tiara', *169*; *lancifolia*, 104; *montana* 'Aureomarginata', *93*, 148, 216; 'Shade Fanfare', 74, 136, *196*, 201, *201*; *sieboldiana*, 121; 'Sum and Sub-stance', 117, 120; *undulata* 'Albo-marginata', 70, 72, *125*

"Hot" colors, *10, 22*, 165–166

Houttuynia cordata 'Chameleon', 76

Hue, use of term, 22
Humulus lupulus 'Aureus', *151*
Hyacinthoides: hispanica, 41, 131; *non-scripta*, 131
Hydrangea, 28, 137–140
Hydrangea: arborescens 'Annabelle', *152;* 'Ayesha', 139; 'Blue Billow', 139; 'Blue Wave', 138; *macrophylla*, 138; *quercifolia*, 193, *194*
Hypericum: androsaemum, 164; fron-dosum, 158; 'Hidcote', *85;* x *moser-ianum* 'Tricolor', 78, *169; tomentosum*, 88
Hypoestes 'Pink Splash', 83
Hyssopus officinalis, 160

Iberis, umbellata, 60, *182*
Ilex: cornuta 'Burfordii', 43; *crenata*, 85, *190*, 198, 218; *verticillata* 'Red Sprite', 193; *vomitoria* 'Nana', 85
Impatiens, 83, *169*
Ipheion uniflorum 'Graystone White', 71
Ipomoea batatas, 105–106
Iris, *23, 38*, 39–40, *40*, 61, 72, 88, *122*, 136, *196;* 'Dewful', 133, *133;* 'Mar-riage Vows', *50;* 'Sahara', *155;* 'Summer Skies', *135*
Iris: fulva, 211; *pallida* 'Variegata', 38, 193, *193*, 204; *pseudacorus, 23*, 72, 76, *130*, 211; *sibirica, 30*, 181; *tecto-rum* 'Variegatum', 200, *202; versico-lor*, 211; 'White Knight', *101*
Isotoma, 136
Ivy, 49, 69, 145–146, 184

Japanese azalea 'Stewartsonianum', *168*
Japanese bleeding heart, *125*
Japanese holly, 85
Japanese iris, *40*, 158
Japanese painted fern, *95*, 105
Japanese sweet flag, 72
Japanese weeping love grass, 208
Jessamine, *196*, 203, 208
Johnny-jump-ups, 57, *57*
Juniper, *46*, 47, 74, 102, *142*
Juniperus davurica, 74

Kale, ornamental 'Peacock', 42
Kerria japonica, 14, 36, *206, 207, 208, 209*, 211, 212, 215, *217*
Kiwi vine, 79, 81
Knautia macedonica, 63, 115
Kniphofia, 159, 192, *192*
Korean chrysanthemum, *218*

Laburnum, *142*
Lad's-love, 105
Lady's mantle, *152*
Lagerstroemia fauriei, 46, 47
Lamb's ears, 37, 116, *116*, 117, 120, *176*
Lamiastrum 'Herman's Pride', *69*
Lamium: maculatum 'Roseum', *173;* 'White Nancy', 68
Language of color, 15–33
Lantana: camara 'Spreading Sunset', *163; trifolia*, 188
Larkspur, *80*, 127, *182*
Lathyrus: chlorantha 'Lemonade', 151; *latifolius, 175*
Laurentia fluviatilis, 136
Lavatera 'Barnsley', *13*
Lavender, *116, 118, 134, 137*, 138
Lawson's cypress, 102
Lenten rose, 104, *173*
Lespedeza thunbergii 'White Fountain', 71
Lettuce, purple, 106–107
Leycesteria formosa, 112
Liatris, *122*
Liatris: 'Kobold', 81, *177; microphylla*, 187
Ligularia tussilaginea 'Argentea', *95*
Ligustrum ovalifolium 'Aureum', *144*
Lilies, 61, *72*, 79, *85, 200*, 212
Lilium: 'Anaconda', *200*, 204; 'Beo-wulf', 114; 'Brushstroke', *60;* 'Ca-sablanca', *122*, 124, *126;* 'Cream Tiger', *200;* 'Enchantment', *90;* 'Flirt', 60; *martagon*, 112, 114, 124; 'Othello', 61–62, 79; *philippinense*, 127; *pumilum*, 215; *regale*, 124; 'Thunderbolt', *200, 202*, 204
Limnanthes douglasii, 155
Linum: narbonense, 136; *perenne*, 136
Liriope: japonica, 68; 'Monroe's

White', 68; *muscari, 82, 83*, 136, 144, 148, *196*, 200
Lobelia: cardinalis, 133, 162; *siphilitica*, 133
Lobularia maritima, 13, 60, *122*
Lonicera: heckrottii, 30, 177; *nitida* 'Baggesen's Gold', *145, 148*, 149; *sempervirens*, 207, *211*
Love-in-a-mist, *53*, 140
Love-lies-bleeding, 76
Luminosity, use of term, 22
Lunaria annua 'Variegata', 61
Lupinus, texensis, 131, 132
Lychnis: x *arkwrightii* 'Vesuvius', *90; coronaria, 23*, 36, *190*
Lyme grass, *101*
Lysimachia: ciliata 'Purpurea', *110*, 111, 112; *nummularia* 'Aurea', 73, *74*, 91, 141, *144, 148*, 213, *214, 215*
Lythrum: 'Morden's Pink', 87, 177; *salicaria*, 37, 177

Madonna lily, 124
Magnolia, 45, 186
Mahonia 'Arthur Menzies', 82, *82*
Mallow, 37, *182*, 183
Malva: moschata, 37; *sylvestris*, 183
Manettia cordifolia, 146, 211
Maples, 43, 77–78, *105*, 108, 153
Marigolds, 91, 94, 168
Marrubium cyllenium, 183
Martagon lily, 112, 114, 124
Massing, 8–9, *9*, 131, *184*
Matteuccia struthiopteris, 104
Mazus reptans 'Alba', 72
Mealycup sage, 122
Meconopsis, 130; *cambrica*, 193
Melianthus major, 120–121
Melissa officinalis 'Allgold', *169*, 198
Mentha longifolia, 183
Mertensia virginica, 131
Mexican orange, 66
Milium effusum "Aureum', *145*, 148, *153*
Mint, 183
Miscanthus, 23, 47, 86–87
Miscanthus sinensis, 43, 44, *45, 75, 92*, 124, *126*, 127, *152, 157*, 208, *219, 220*

Mock oranges, golden, 147
Moluccella laevis, 105
Monarda: 'Adam', 62; 'Blue Stock-
   ing', *176;* 'Cambridge Scarlet', *164;*
   'Colrain Red', *177;* 'Croftway
   Pink', 177; *fistulosa,* 81, 183
Mondo grass, *118,* 183–184, 207
Money plant, 61
Monkshood, 174
Mourning-widow geranium,
   114
Mouse-eared chickweed, 121
Myosotis: scorpioides, 167; *sylvatica,*
   167

Nandina, 150, 207, *219*
Nandina domestica, 82–83, *82*
Narcissus, *124*
Narcissus: 'Ambergate', *209;* 'Flower
   Record', *194;* 'Jet Fire', *209;* 'Little
   Gem', *169;* 'Martha Washington',
   36
Nasturtium, *90*
Neillia thibetica, 112
Nepeta: nervosa, 171; 'Six Hills Giant',
   101
Nicotiana: alata 'Lime Green', 149;
   langsforfii, 149
Nigella: damascena, 53, 140; *hispanica,*
   140
Ninebark, *145*
None-so-pretty, 54, 57

Oak-leaved hydrangeas, 193, *194*
Oenothera: fruticosa, 22; *missouriensis*
   'Greencourt Lemon', 106; *odorata*
   'Sulphurea', *164; speciosa, 56,* 58;
   tetragona riparia, 23, 88; *tetragona*
   'Sonnenwende', 158
Onion, 44, *45,* 63, 186
Onopordum acanthium, 101, 159
Onosma echioides, 204
Ophiopogon, 183–184; *planiscapus*
   'Nigrescens', 108, *118,* 207
Orange gardens, 165–168
Orchid, 28, 54, *55,* 184
Oriental fringe-tree, 127
Origanum: laevigatum, 189; *vulgare*
   'Aureum', 100, *117,* 143, 144, *186,*
   188, 189

Oxalis: brasiliensis, 76; regnellii 'Purpurea', 105; *rubra* 'Alba', 73, *73;*
   triangularis, 105
Oxypetalum caaeruleum, 140

Pachysandra, variegated, *69*
Painted arum, 162
Panicum virgatum 'Heavy Metal', *23,*
   121, *161*
Pansies, *10, 52,* 61, *85,* 107, *144, 174*
Pastel, use of term, 22
Patio rose, 170
Patrinia gibbosa, 150
Pelargonium, *90*
Pelargonium peltatum, 49
Pennisetum: alopecuroides 'Hameln',
   87; *setaceum,* 86; *setaceum atrosangui-*
   neum, 108
Penstemon, *80*
Penstemon: digitalis 'Husker's Red',
   105; *hirsutus,* 189
Peony, *101, 122*
Perilla, *63, 176*
Perilla frutescens 'Crispa', 109, *172, 177*
Periwinkle, 72–73
Perovskia, *176, 177*
Petasites japonicus, 69, 103
Phacelia bipinnatifida, 131
Phalaris arundinacea, 44, *92, 159*
Philadelphus coronarius 'Aureus', 147
Phlomis russeliana, 130
Phlox, 71, *80, 122*
Phlox: amoena, 37; 'David', 71; *divari-*
   cata, 70; 'Miss Lingard', 71; 'Mt.
   Fuji', 71; 'Norah Leigh', *72; panicu-*
   lata, 81, *176; subulata, 31,* 59, *59,*
   129, *178*
Photinia x *fraseri,* 41, *50,* 157, 206
Phuopsis stylosa, 174
Phygelius, 170; 'African Queen', 36,
   164; 'Yellow Trumpet', *99*
Physocarpus opulifolius, 145
Pineapple lily, 105
Pink foliage, 76–79, 81, 83
Pink gardens, 171–181
Placement, *128, 143*
Plantago: major 'Rosularis', 105; *major*
   rubrifolia, 107–108
Platycodons, *176*
Plumbago, 135

Polyanthus, 58
Polygonatum odoratum, 28, 67
Polygonum aubertii, 128
Polystichum polyblepharum, 164
Poor-man's orchid, 60
Poppies, *80,* 130, 140, 162, *162, 164,*
   187, 188, 193
Portulaca oleracea, 158, *159, 194,* 197–
   198
Potato vine, *137*
Potentilla: astrosanguinea, 162; *nepalen-*
   sis 'Miss Willmott', 38–39; *recta*
   'Sulphurea', *199,* 203; 'Roxana', 39;
   thurberi, 43
Pratia pedunculata, 136, 196, 197
Primary colors, 21–22
Primrose, 72, 77–78, 140, *158, 164*
Primula: sieboldii, 39; vulgaris, 78
Prunus: cerasifera, 105, 108; x *cistena,*
   108
Pulmonaria angustifolia, 22
Punctuation, 84–88, *89,* 218
Purple flowers, 181–189
Purple foliage, 105–114
Purple loosestrife, 37, 72, 177
Purple plum, 105
Pyracantha 'Mohave', *46,* 47

Queen Anne's lace, *168*
Quince, 70–71

Ranunculus ficaria 'Brazen Hussy', 90,
   91, 106, *213,* 214–215
Red foliage, *50*
Red gardens, 162–165
Regal lily, *99,* 124
Repetition, 84–88, *93, 134*
Rhazya orientalis, 135
Rhododendron, 69, *86,* 177
Rhododendron prunifolium, 163, 164
Robinia pseudoacacia 'Frisia', 141, *220*
Rock garden, *118*
Rodgersia aesculifolia, 102
Rohdea japonica, 164
Rosa: 'Betty Prior', 59, 171, *178;*
   'Cornelia', 41; *glauca (rubrifolia),*
   62, 108, 111, 112; 'Graham
   Thomas', *194,* 197; 'Mary Rose',
   159, 160, *160;* 'Mutabilis', 111; 'Pe-
   tite Pink', *179; roxburghii, 159,* 160;

rubrifolia, 114; *rugosa*, 112, *175*; 'Veilchenblau', 183

Rose: 'Apricot Nectar', 170; 'Ballerina', 79; 'Cardinal de Richelieu', 37; 'Cerise Bouquet', *181*; 'Helen Knight', *155*; 'Othello', 37; 'Sweet Dream', 170; 'Sweet Juliet', 170; 'William Lobb', 37

Rose plantain, 105

Rosinweed, *157*

Rudbeckia: maxima, 121, *190*; *nitida* 'Herbstsonne', *157*; *triloba*, 217

Ruellia: humilis, 133; *strepens*, 133

Rumex sanguineus, 106

Ruta graveolens, 99, 121, *190*

Sage, 76–77, 77, 122, 166

Sagina subulata 'Aurea', 73, 141, 143, *152*

Salix: alba, 43, *119*; *purpurea*, 107, *110*, 111, 112

Salvia: argentea, 117, 120, 121; *azurea*, 133, 135; *coccinea*, 127, 166; 'East Friesland', 105, *176*; *farinacea*, *122*, *128*; *guaranitica*, 136, 139; 'Indigo Spires', 139, *176*; *leucantha*, 46; 'May Night', 58; *officinalis*, 76–77, 77, *85*, 111; x *superba*, 88, 183; *urticifolia*, 171; *vanhouttei*, *179*; *viridis* (*horminum*), 79

Sambucus nigra 'Guincho Purple', 108–109

Sand cherry, 108

Sanguisorba: canadensis, 174; *tenuifolia purpurea*, 114

Santolina, *116*, 155

Santolina: chamaecyparissus, 121; 'Edward Bowles', 197

Sanvitalia procumbens, *90*

Scabiosa, 115; *ochroleuca*, 192, *192*, *195*

Scarlet gardens, 165–166

Schizanthus, 60–61

Scilla, 131; *hispanica*, 41; *scilloides*, 20

Scotch moss, 73, 143, *152*, 215

Scotch thistle, *101*, *159*

Secondary colors, 21–22

Sedges, 68, 70, 76, 115, 121, 148–149

Sedum: aizoon, 203; *alboroseum* 'Mediovariegatum', 88–90, *89*, 100, 136, 193, *193*; 'Autumn Joy', *168*,

174; 'Bertram Anderson', 107; *lineare* 'Variegatum', 184; 'Ruby Glow', 107; *spurium* 'Dragon's Blood', *88*; 'Vera Jameson', 107, 111; 'Weihenstephaner Gold', 42, 87

Self-echoes, 58–61, *182*

Self-sowing plants, 54, *55*, 57–58, *57*, *95*, 166, *210*

Selinum tenuifolium, *102*

Sempervivum, *52*

Senna, *157*

Serendipity, 54–58, *54*

Shade, use of term, 22

Shasta daisy, *75*, *126*

Shrub rose, *181*

Shrubs, blue-flowered, 136–138; stoloniferous, 44

Siberian iris, 133, *133*, 135, *135*

Silene: armeria, 11; *polypetala*, 180; *virginica*, 54, 57, 180

Silphium perfoliatum, 157

Silver lace vine, 128

Silver willow, *119*

Sisyrinchium, *38*

Sisyrinchium californicum, *196*

Skunk cabbage, *104*

Smokebush, *101*, 108, 110, 112, *113*

Smyrnium perfoliatum, 143

Snapdragon, *85*, *176*

Snowdrop, 69

Solanum crispum, *137*

Solidago: 'Golden Mosa', *156*; *verna*, *12*

Solidaster x *hybridus*, 192

Solomon's seal, 28, 67

Sorrel, 106

Space: and cohesion, 95; and contrast, *92*, 94

Spanish bluebells, 41, 131

Spectral colors, 21, 24

Spiraea: 'Gold Mound', *147*; *japonica*, 37, *65*, 84, 94, *145*, 167, *205*, *206*, 211, *212–213*, *219*; *nipponica* 'Snowmound', *30*; 'Shirobana', 114

Stachys: byzantina, 37, 115, 116, *117*, 120, *176*; *coccinea*, 39

Starflower, 71

Stems, echoes in, 41–42, 43

Sternbergia lutea, 7

Stipa gigantea, *64*

Structure and ornament, 47–54

Styrax, 45; *japonica*, 68

Sun: and colors, 27–28, 109, 110; and heat, 120, 143, 153

Sundrops, 22, *23*, 88

Sunflowers, 155

Surprise, 155

Sweet alyssum, *13*, 60, *122*

Sweet flag, 67

Sweet william, 33, 114, 171, 174

Sweet woodruff, 69, *70*, *96*, 104

Symphytum: grandiflorum, 40–41, *193*; x *uplandicum*, 192, *192*

Symplocarpus foetidus, *104*

Tagetes: patula 'Espano Granada', *163*; *tenuifolia*, 91, 94

Tanacetum densum amani, *119*, 121

Taxus bacatta 'Standishii', 67, *67*

Teucrium chamaedrys, *96*

Texas bluebonnets, *131*, 132

Thalictrum: aquilegifolium, 65; *speciosissimum*, 159

Thermopsis villosa, 87

Threadleaf cypress, 97

Thyme, *137*, *152*; creeping, *158*; golden, 36, *143*, *190*, 200; woolly, *13*, *118*, *119*, 121

Thymus pseudolanuginosus, *13*, *118*, *119*, 121

Tint, use of term, 22

Tone, use of term, 22

Torch lily, *159*, 192, *192*

Tovara 'Painter's Palette', 83–84

Trachelospermum asiaticum 'Variegatum', 66

Tradescantia, 88

Trailing verbena, 58–59

Tropaeolum tuberosum, 146

Trumpet honeysuckle, 207, *217*

Tsuga canadensis 'Gentsch White', 49

Tulip, *21*, *52*, 61, *65*, *94*, *144*; 'Ad Rem', *208*; 'Angel', 66–67, *66*; 'Angelique', *178*; 'The Bishop', *184*; 'Golden Artist', 66; 'Greenland', 66; lily-flowered, 48, *125*; 'New Design', *31*; 'Oriental Splendour', *10*; 'Oxford's Elite', *10*;

Tulip (*cont.*)

   'Queen of Sheba', *14, 205, 206, 208,* 212; 'Spring Green', 66, 67; 'Unsurpassable', *184;* viridiflora, 66; 'White Triumphator', *48, 125*

Tulipa: kaufmanniana, 43; *maximo-wiczii,* 100–101; *pulchella* 'Persian Pearl', 76

Ulmus parviflora, 46
Unity, 5, *80,* 97–101
Upside-down-flower, 104

Value, use of term, 22
Vancouveria, 104
Verbascum, 40, *40, 116*
Verbascum: bombyciferum, 13; nigrum, 164
Verbena, 88, 112, *134,* 158
Verbena: bonariensis, 176, 187, 188, *199;* 'Lavender', *134, 159, 160;* 'Silver Anne', *30,* 157, *159,* 171; *tenu-*

isecta, 23, 183, 187; 'Texas Form', 58–59; 'Violet Purple', 185–186, *186*
Veronica, 88; 'Goodness Grows', *178; prostrata* 'Trehane', 144, 200; *spicata, 122, 176;* 'Sunny Border Blue', 136
Veronicastrum virginicum, 124
Vinca minor, 72–73
Viola: labradorica (riviniana 'Purpurea'), 108; *tricolor,* 17, 57–58, *57, 213,* 214, *215*
Viper's bugloss, 132, 158
Virginia bluebells, 131
Vitis vinifera 'Purpurea', 107

Wallflower, 57, *57*
Warminster broom, 74
Wax begonias, 83
Weather: and blues, 132; and changing light, 27–28

Weigela florida, 60, 96, 108, 112, *153*
White foliage echoes, 23, *31,* 68–73, *69*
White gardens, *72,* 91, 100, 122–129, *122*
Willow, 43–45, 107, 111, *119, 154*
Winter, 43, 82–83, 84–85
Woolly thyme, *13, 118, 119,* 121

Yarrow, *62,* 94
Yellow flag iris, *23, 72*
Yellow gardens, *12,* 154–161, *154, 155, 156, 157*
Yews, 102
Yucca: 'Bright Edge', *46,* 213, 218, *219; filamentosa* 'Variegata', *31,* 58, 71; *glauca,* 121; 'Golden Sword', 47

Zephyranthes candida, 71
Zinnias, *172*